D0560353

DISCARDED

WHO ARE WE?

261
Els

WHO ARE WE?

Critical Reflections
and Hopeful Possibilities

JEAN BETHKE ELSHTAIN

17606

William B. Eerdmans Publishing Company

Grand Rapids, Michigan / Cambridge, U.K.

© 2000 Wm. B. Eerdmans Publishing Co.

255 Jefferson Ave. S.E., Grand Rapids, Michigan 49503 /

P.O. Box 163, Cambridge CB3 9PU U.K.

All rights reserved

Printed in the United States of America

05 04 03 02 01 00   7 6 5 4 3 2 1

Library of Congress Cataloging-in-Publication Data

Elshtain, Jean Bethke, 1941-

Who are we?: critical reflections and hopeful possibilities / Jean Bethke Elshtain.

p.   cm.

Originally prepared for the 1998 Hein-Fry lecture series.

ISBN 0-8028-3888-X (alk. paper)

1. Man (Christian theology).

2. Bonhoeffer, Dietrich, 1906-1945.

3. John Paul II, Pope, 1920-

I. Title.

BT701.2.E47 2000

261 — dc21

99-462191

The author and publisher gratefully acknowledge the following publications, in which these poems by Fred Ding first appeared:

"Claims of the Past" and "The Force of Intent" in *Tri Quarterly*

"Letter to Genetically Engineered Super-Humans" in *Poetry* (March 1996)

"II. Matthew 6:9-13" in *The New Republic*

To my colleagues
at the University of Chicago Divinity School

Contents

Preface: Caveats and Gratitude   ix

Introduction: Who Are We?   3

Chapter One: How Far Have We Fallen?   7

Chapter Two: Forgetting That We Are Fallen:
The Prideful Self   39

Chapter Three: Forgetting That We Are Fallen:
The Slothful Self   81

Conclusion: Living in Hope   127

Index   171

Preface

Caveats and Gratitude

How much should an author reveal at a book's beginning of what the reader will have discerned for him- or herself by book's end? Mulling this over, I determined that it would be helpful to readers to explain why a social and political theorist is tending to matters theological. I am not a systematic theologian; rather, I approach the daunting and complex issues taken up in the pages to follow from a perspective that freely mingles theological, ethical, philosophical, and political categories and concerns. This means placing within a single frame arguments drawn from texts with which I have long engaged from the history of Western thought, to which are added theological works I haven't labored over so intensely for as long.[1] My education in

---

1. I don't mean to suggest that I have simply ignored theological thinkers in the past. My first book, *Public Man, Private Woman: Women in Social and Political Thought* (Princeton: Princeton University Press, 1981; second ed. 1992), took up Augustine, Aquinas, and Luther. My other books, including *Women and War,* feature discussions of works in theology and Christian ethics. But it must be said that this is not what political theorists usually do, in large part because the key texts are not taught and because "religion" is labeled one thing, "politics" another.

theology is largely informal. I have been reading St. Augustine since I was eighteen years old, but not for the purposes of any course or seminar. If and when Augustine appeared in political theory courses, he had a brief walk-on role in Act Two ("medieval political thought") based largely on excerpts labeled "theological." They were either conspicuous by their absence or conspicuously assigned to lesser roles in the great scheme of things.

This rigid separation of theology and politics — a division on a level of thought somewhat akin to the "wall" between church and state advanced by one dominant strand of American jurisprudence — meant that thinkers who ought not to have been set apart were sundered and that fruitful and important engagements did not occur. This, at least, is my gloss on the story of political theory training in American higher education.

I now have the opportunity, given my academic setting, to draw together in a more sustained and robust manner my lifelong informal engagement with theology and my formal training in political thought. Matters that were often residual or implicit in my work are now surfacing in an explicit and detailed way. Whether I am doing a good job of doing this is, of course, not for me to judge. But my theological turn dovetails with my long held view that we must tend explicitly to the reigning descriptions and vocabularies under which our activities — as persons, communities, and cultures — go forward. Some descriptions of our capacities, our activities, and our worlds not only exclude other vocabularies but may impoverish rather than enrich our understanding of the world, including our gifts for complex discernments. Much of the burden of argument in *Who Are We?* is borne along by interpreting and assessing contrasting descriptive vocabularies in light of the normative claims and ordering of goods and possibilities these *necessarily* underscore, emphasize, and urge upon us.

As I was moving through the exercises that follow, I was struck all over again by just how unfortunate it is, first, that political theory got severed from theology and much of philosophy and, second, that political theory got marginalized in the academic study of politics in the United States. Political and social theorists often find themselves isolated, if not embattled, in departments of political science. How so? Because what these theorists do and how they do it is not the thing that is supposed to be done if one is devoted to the "scientific" study of politics. I will not here rehearse the systematic essays, chapters in books, and portions of books I have devoted to this controversial claim in the past.[2] But this much needs mentioning: In limiting our descriptive vocabularies to the presuppositions of "behaviorism," or the now pervasive "rational choice" perspective, we radically simplify to the point of reductionism our treatment of persons and their worlds. If everything human beings say and do is, in principle, decoctable to the "bottom line" of utility maximization, much of what human beings say and do will remain unintelligible to us.

That, at least, is what I will be arguing in my treatment of both economic concerns in Chapter Two and highly voluntaristic (and thus skewed and distorted) views of human freedom in Chapter Three. The routine separation of "description" and "evaluation" within the positivistic schema that underwrite the once regnant behaviorism and the new triumphant rational choice approaches rules out unpacking the evaluations imbedded within our descriptive vocabularies, *including* those deployed by behaviorists and rational choice thinkers. Descriptions are never merely neutral, with evaluation reduced to second-

2. See, for example, Jean Bethke Elshtain, "Methodological Sophistication and Conceptual Confusion," in *Real Politics: At the Center of Everyday Life* (Baltimore: Johns Hopkins University Press, 1997), pp. 12-35. This is a reprint of an essay that appeared originally in 1979 and is devoted to a critique of the presuppositions underlying the then dominant behaviorist school in political science.

order activity in the form of "biases" or "subjective preferences" that are not rationally defensible. But if one embraces the "neutralist" way, facts are reduced to brute data and our descriptions can no longer serve as a source of moral or ethical information, or one denies that the terms of discourse one *must* employ just to say anything bear any normative import.

Consider one brief example. The word "person" or those two words "human being" do more — much more — than just point to a spatio-temporal entity of a certain sort like armadillo or tree, something that can be picked out and identified. Not at all. These simple words — "person" or "human being" — when used to name a being of a certain sort, already constitute a commitment of a certain kind. It is altogether unsurprising that when the tormenters of humankind launch their dirty work, they begin by changing the language. Some persons are no longer to be described as human beings. Knowing that this characterization bears a normative load, the tormenters know that their job is made much easier if they are successful in characterizing persons in ways that deny or detract from their humanity. Persons are described as "animals" or "parasites" or "vermin," and the moral and ethical imperatives imbedded in a particular description are lost or altered.

As I argue in Chapter Four, when words implode, so do worlds. We need as many complex terms as we can muster to help us do the hard work of trying to "get it right" by describing the world with sufficient complexity and nuance that we come as close as our fallible minds will take us to the stuff of reality itself: that out of which we are made and that which, in turn, helps us to become what we already are — persons — and therefore beings of a certain kind who can be assaulted and damaged and whose lives and cultures can be badly distorted or deformed or, contrastingly, whose lives and cultures can be amplified capaciously in the direction of respect for human dignity. We can live in hope through God's grace, we beings who pass away. Here the theological perspective is crucial in helping us to treat the question of human appearance and human living and human passing away in and through time. Political theorists are most often preoccupied with political spaces — the *polis,* the *civitas,* the nation-state. But theologians grapple with the coming into being and passing away of lives, and they conjure, therefore, with the multiple meanings of these passings *sub specie aeternitatis.* From a theological perspective, things look much different than they do if we have privileged one particular sort of human arrangement — like the sovereign state — and made it the source of overriding if not exhaustive value. There is so much vitality and vibrancy within the great works that constitute the tradition of Western Christian theology, including the concepts and categories with which we can challenge that very tradition, that it is a self-inflicted wound of a particularly grave sort to ignore, jettison, or even scorn that tradition.[3]

Happily (for me), dialogue around the primary preoccupations of the political theorist is central, not peripheral, to our enterprise in Swift Hall, the home of the Divinity School at the Univeristy of Chicago. For that I am enormously grateful. It has emboldened me to go public in a serious way with the fruits of my own theological engagements. The specific occasions for this text were the Hein-Fry Lectures of 1998. The brochure put out by the Division of Ministry of the Evangelical Lutheran Church in America describes the Hein-Fry Lecture Series as one that "identifies lively, pressing theological issues facing the church and offers lectures that stimulate intellectual inquiry and discussion of those issues at eight seminaries of the church." The goals

---

3. This is not, of course, a covert claim that the tradition of Western theological and religious thinking is the *only* vital tradition. Of course not. But it is the only one I know enough about to discuss intelligibly.

of this endowed series are to encourage and to foster scholarship and dialogue. I am enormously grateful to the ELCA and the Hein-Fry Lecture Series Governing Committee for selecting me to be a Hein-Fry lecturer in 1998. The overall theme given by the committee to the lecturer was: "The Ethical Challenges of the New Century: How Do Christians Respond?" I learned much in the writing of these lectures — now book chapters — and in their delivery. The questions put to me at the four seminaries I visited — Martha Stortz, the other lecturer for 1998, also visited four seminaries — entered into the revisions I made for purposes of publication. It has long been my view that thinking is inherently a dialogical enterprise, one that requires multiple interlocutors, and in that, too, I have been lucky. I especially want to thank Reinhard Hütter, Duke Divinity School, who was a member of the Hein-Fry Committee, for his support and for his helpful suggestions concerning publication.

There is one other matter that must detain us for just a moment, namely, the question of tone or style — at base a rhetorical issue. I recall here a conversation a small company of us had with President Václav Havel of the Czech Republic in the fall of 1992. President Havel was asked, by one among us, a question more or less along these lines: "When I read your essays and then turn to your plays, I have the sense of reading two entirely different authors. How do you square the moral earnestness of one with the ironic tone of the other?" Havel more or less replied: "It is the same man, but different occasions." This is a pithy, shorthand way of drawing our attention to rhetorical occasions. Some modes of discourse and genres are more suited to certain occasions than to others. In the Christian tradition, one finds a wonderful variety of tones and modes, from the jeremiad to the epistle to the parable to the sermon to the systematic treatise to the prayer to the hymn — on and on.

Here are my specific considerations for the purpose of this

text. I have long worried that, from time to time, those who embrace the powerful term *prophetic* for their work use it as a kind of ideological cover. "Prophetic" too often seems to amount to denunciatory rhetoric attached to a specific political agenda. In such cases, the hard scholarly work is frequently shirked. I mention this because I detect a certain prophetic urgency at work in this text, although I would never claim the mantle "prophet" for myself and I trust that I have done the necessary scholarly work responsibly. I believe, with Dietrich Bonhoeffer, that we are obliged to ask: What is to come? Where are the powerful tendencies and forces at century's end pushing us? What can we do about it?

One of my frustrations, as theorist and citizen, is the fact that those who remain wedded to a strong progressivist teleology, certain sorts of liberals, often foresee *only* the most benign possible outcomes of social reform or of the forces at work that they can associate with "progressive" forward motion. In this way, thinkers in the American context, including a number of the turn-of-the-century Social Gospelers as well as their contemporary heirs, were and are immunized against what Reinhold Niebuhr called the ironies of American history; or what others, in more social-science language, call the unintended consequences of change. By contrast, a certain kind of conservative may see only malign possibilities in any and all strong efforts to alter things knowingly and perhaps even dramatically; and that attitude, if pervasive, constitutes a negation of human freedom. If the teleological "progressivist-liberal" sees no principled limits to change, to gaining more control over nature, and so on, the stalwart conservative shrinks from any strenuous projects that call on human ingenuity and creative energy. So carving out the in-between seems to me a vital task, by which I mean finding decent, substantively defended limits to freedom, yet underscoring our capacity to act and our duty to act responsibly. That is the terrain I hope I have sketched in this work. No doubt I have gone off course from time to time but I hope not too often and not too egregiously. The reader must be the judge.

Clearly, this work should be seen as of a piece with my political theory writings, not as a radical departure of any kind. Perhaps *Augustine and the Limits of Politics* (1996) marks a turning point toward explicitly theological concerns. But, from my first book, *Public Man, Private Woman: Women in Social and Political Thought,* to this most recent effort, my abiding themes have always been ethical. The driving motive behind the concluding chapter of *Public Man, Private Woman* is a vision of an "ethical polity." I say this because I think a scholarly career is the slow unfolding of our most central and defining themes and preoccupations. We may play up one angle for one purpose, a different slant for another. But all of it fits together in what would be a rather rough-hewn patchwork quilt were all the pieces to be stitched together in order to make explicit the whole that had been there all along.

I plead guilty to the fact that my tone is frequently ironic and that a few of my observations and barbs are tinged with a bit of what I like to think of as wit but others might see as too cheeky. There is not much I can do about that. It is the way I write. At least I can state, honestly, that I am sedate by comparison to Martin Luther! I do think we have an obligation to be as lively with our prose as we can in order to draw readers in and to hold their attention. Vivid examples are a help, as are occasional homey references. We cannot breathe if the air is too relentlessly and persistently rarified. This is not a brief against systematic theology or philosophy. I find reading Karl Barth's *Church Dogmatics,* for example, a task in which I am an amateur although I hope to become more seasoned, an exhilarating experience. The same holds for the two primary interlocutors for this work, Dietrich Bonhoeffer and John Paul II. Systematic theology often has its own kind of poetry, and such moments pop out frequently in the writings of Bonhoeffer and John Paul II.

Let me conclude by thanking my family for rooting me in the world and helping me to understand God's great goodness in creating us for deep and loving relationships. Sometimes when I look at our grandchildren — JoAnn Paulette Welch, Christopher Matthew Welch, and Robert Paul Bethke — they are, to me, so beautiful and so extraordinary and so palpably reflective of creation's goodness that it brings tears to my eyes. I hope this gratitude at created being has worked its way into the very tissue of these reflections.

CLAIMS OF THE PAST

What if we could find a way to sift
the winds for drifting minds to place in bodies
again? Whom would we choose and why? The saviors

and philosopher kings to stop our squabbling? the poor
who choked in obscurity and filth? the nameless
heroes who sacrificed themselves? the murdered,

the stifled, the unfulfilled? the evil to repair
their shame? the children who barely had a chance?
Who, among all the unredeemed

billions swirling like leaves to be reborn,
wouldn't have some claim for living more?
Isn't it better the dead come back as they do,

briefly, when they surface in a stranger's face
or voice or in a scrap of song, or steadily,
when light shafts through a window in an empty room

and the motes of dust almost coalesce,
or suddenly, when memories storm our solitude
in vacant lots or crowds, clouding us

in pain or refreshing us in a rinse of remembrance,
leaving everything shining, veneered with past,
and perhaps valued more because it does not last.

FRED DINGS,
from *Eulogy for a Private Man*
(reprinted with permission of the author)

If evil appears in the form of light, beneficence, loyalty and renewal, if it conforms with historical necessity and social justice, this, if it is understood straightforwardly, is a clear additional proof of its abysmal wickedness. But the moral theorist is blinded by it. With the concepts he already has in mind he is unable to grasp what is real and still less able to come seriously to grips with that of which the essence and power are entirely unknown to him.

DIETRICH BONHOEFFER

This, my dear ones, is the great and universal community of all Christians, of the whole Church, of all of us who on this night live once again the birth of God into this world. We break and share bread, exchanging the same wishes as those expressed by the angels that night in Bethlehem: "Glory to God in the highest, and peace on earth to men of goodwill."

Tonight we are all of us overwhelmed and dumbfounded in the face of the divine love which took on human flesh and entered into the human spirit. We compare our miserable human love with his immeasurable love, and we pray that love may grow within us, that it may never be extinguished despite any difficulties or obstacles, and that it may never dim but always grow stronger.

KAROL WOJTYLA
Archbishop of Krakow,
Midnight Mass, 1969

Who Are We?

In the terrible days of his confinement in Tegel, a Gestapo prison, and before his martyrdom, Dietrich Bonhoeffer commenced on an activity that surprised his dear and good friend, Eberhard Bethge: he began to write poetry — this in addition to his letters to family and friends, his theological arguments, and even a foray or two into fiction. One poem is entitled "Who Am I?"

> They also tell me
> I would bear the days of my misfortune
> equally, smilingly, proudly,
> like one accustomed to win.
> Am I then really all that? . . .
> Or am I only what I know of myself,
> restless and longing and sick, like a bird in a cage,
> struggling for breath, as though hands were
>   compressing my throat,
> yearning for colours, for flowers, for the voices of birds,
> thirsting for words of kindness, for neighbourliness . . .
> powerlessly trembling for friends at an infinite distance,

weary and empty at praying, at thinking, at making,
faint, and ready to say farewell to it all?
Who am I?

He answers in a way that seems entirely foreign to the vast majority of late-twentieth-century Americans: "Whoever I am, thou
knowest, O God, I am thine."

I am *thine*. I am not my own. We no longer believe any such
thing. Indeed, such a pronouncement — I am not sovereign in
my own domain; I am a creature; I am not simply the sum total
of my choices; I am tempest-tossed; I am not in full control; I am
unsure of what I will do tomorrow — these sorts of pronounce-
ments make us candidates for assertiveness training and other
interventions and ministrations designed to bolster an obviously
weak, even sick, "self-image." For we have no other way to think
of humility than as perverse self-abnegation.

Who, then, are we, we prideful late-twentieth-century creatures? Lord knows, we no longer think of ourselves as *belonging*
to anyone or anything. We do not belong — we own; we possess.
And that, to say the least, is not the same thing. We plunge into
self-aggrandizement convinced that the dazzling success of our
projects will prove definitely who we are. But this fails to satisfy.
Our triumphs ring hollow. Our victories so often turn to ashes in
our mouths. But never mind. Tomorrow we will run faster, climb
higher, and one fine morning. . . . Who are we? We are creatures
who have forgotten what it means to be faithful to something
other than ourselves.

I offer three exercises in interpretive faithfulness. I propose to
tap the wellsprings of the Christian tradition, or features of that
tradition that I know best, primarily, though not exclusively,
through several of its most extraordinary exemplars. What does
the Christian tradition offer? How does this tradition connect to
the lives we are now living? For a living faith exudes performative

consequences; it instructs us on how to live; it enlivens the very sinews of our being. There is a word to describe what I am to be about: *ressourcement:* tapping the great, replenishing sources, the ever fresh waters of a living tradition. This is not a return in the sense of an originary quest. We cannot get behind the back of history. We cannot go back to reproduce a pristine moment.

Despite my disclaimer, there are those who insist that any attempt to root ourselves in a tradition precisely in order to release the vibrancy of that tradition is a forlorn exercise in nostalgia. Some speak scathingly of timorous souls given to "declinism" rather than to a robust embrace of contemporary culture in all its dizzying multiform complexity. But this is often jejune, a way to evade rather than to confront the perplexities of the present and that past yet present to it. No complex tradition is ever exhausted. By contrast, many trumpeted yet simplistic practices and slogans and reassurances of the current moment are exhausted — or so I shall argue — and thus those who adhere to these practices and the ideologies that animate them are ill equipped to help us hack our way through the dense thicket of our time. And I use the ungainly word *hack* advisedly. There is never a clear, smooth superhighway laid out before us. To be sure, we may convince ourselves of such — as, for example, the techno-boosters of the present moment who promise perfect gleaming futures once we have cleared up various glitches, including the imperfection coded into the stuff we call human — but they are wrong. Perhaps we are in the midst of the situation Bonhoeffer described as a moment in which would-be angels of light cannot see the flaws in their own culture's projects, even to the point of collusion with the forces of darkness.

But let us not move to such a mordant conclusion too quickly, for Christians are enjoined to live in hope. I see these exercises as a moment of critical hopefulness made possible by faithfulness. Hopefulness truly helps to open the windows —

and we have a word for that, too, *aggiornamento* — to the fresh breezes that might bestir us yet. For we are created to "serve God wittily, in the tangle of our minds," as Thomas More declares in Robert Bolt's play *A Man for All Seasons*. To serve God wittily, not glumly. With replenishment and renewal. It is not true, as is sometimes claimed, that our ethics is behind the times and has failed to catch up with the radical transformations of the present. No, rather, the problem is: we are not using the ethics that we have, especially we communities of belief that embody a tradition the culture long ago abandoned. Let us think again, then, what it means to be taught that we must lose ourselves for the Lord's sake. What self is to be lost? And what do we thereby gain?

Chapter One

How Far Have We Fallen?

As we reach the end of this bloodiest of centuries, we find ourselves taking stock. Where have we been? Where are we going? What are our prospects? Who are we? Human beings have long been preoccupied with these questions. In the dark 1982 film *Bladerunner* (loosely based on science fiction writer Phillip K. Dick's book, *Do Androids Dream of Electric Sheep?*), a bladerunner — a man given a license to hunt down and to kill advanced androids called replicants — comes up against the most advanced replicant model. This particular model is extraordinarily precise, very intelligent, very powerful, and capable of great violence. The only way to distinguish a replicant from a human being is to put the replicant through a series of tests that monitor pupil dilation as the respondent answers queries like: "You are walking along on a hot day. The sun is beating down. You see a turtle lying upside down, unable to turn over. What do you do?"

A human being will register something on the empathy scale — discernible through pupil change — to such a query, but the replicant, being deficient in this quality, will not. For replicants are manufactured, not begotten. They have an "incept date" rather than a birthday. They have not gone through a process of education of the moral faculties. As well, they are programmed to die — or to wear out — on another foreordained date determined by their manufacturer. They have no families, but their manufacturer has implanted memories. So they believe they had families and childhoods like other human beings. But this, too, proves to be false. When the replicants finally realize this deception, they come to hate their manufacturer. Replicants also know they are being hunted as the flaw in their design — the failure on the empathic scale — makes them quite dangerous. So they live in perpetual fear. The dilemma is that by being implanted with a past, however fraudulent, the replicants have come closer and closer to us — or at least to what we once believed we were until we decided that we might actually be history-less, by which I mean undetermined by anything that went before. But I jump ahead of the story.

The bladerunner, Deckard, played by Harrison Ford, is assigned to hunt down and kill a renegade band of replicants who have escaped from interplanetary servitude. He does so systematically and bloodily, one by one. Rachel, an advanced replicant who never left the office of her manufacturer and works there as an assistant in a dying and decaying Earth, who is not, therefore, a member of the replicant rebel band, seems way too close to us for comfort. Deckard tests her and realizes that she is a replicant; and this knowledge torments him. For Rachel, too, is in the danger zone, as Deckard can kill any and all replicants, whether they are marauding or not. Learning from Deckard that her implanted memories are false, Rachel weeps. What is this? Replicants are not supposed to have feelings. Has she somehow transcended replicant-being to join human-being? Deckard, recognizing at one point that he cannot kill her because she has helped to save him when one of the horrifically violent renegade replicants was preparing to gouge his eyes out and because he has fallen in love with her, plunges into dark self-doubt. What about Rachel? Rachel weeping, weeping not for her children but for her own nonchildhood, her nonhuman-being.

There is a final encounter with the head of the outlaw replicant band, Roy. Roy is dying, or, in replicant-being, wearing out. His expiration day is upon him. He howls at the universe and at his manufacturer, howls as he feels himself inexorably, inevitably running down. He pierces a palm with a nail, a kind of crucifixion, because the pain helps him to feel life until the very end. In the terrible struggle with Deckard, Roy gets the better of Deckard, who clings to the ledge of a building and, as he loses his grip and will surely plunge to an awful death, Roy, the replicant with no feeling, reaches out, from his great if waning strength, and pulls Deckard to the safety of the building top on which their deadly *pas de deux* now reaches its denouement in the year of our Lord, 2019. Roy tells Deckard his story: about what it is like to be a slave and to live in fear. About all the sights he has seen, moments that will "be lost in time like tears in the rain. Time to die." He expires and a white dove he has captured is released and flutters into the besmirched, acid-rain-filled sky.

A soul freed? We do not know. Deckard offers up a commentary. He tries to understand why this violent, nonfeeling entity has spared him. "Maybe he loved life more in these last moments, anybody's life, my life." He concludes: "All he wanted is what we all want. Where do I come from? Where am I going? How long have I got?" Transformed through this experience, Deckard abandons his terrible profession and flees with Rachel. The film ends with this voice-over: "I didn't know how long we'd have together. Who does?"[1] Few of us can live with such uncertainty. But all of us must. Or at least we used to believe that we must. But increasingly

1. The version of *Bladerunner* here discussed is the original version released to the public. The later "Director's cut" version is longer and has no narration. I much prefer the earlier, narrated film. Ford's voice is subtle and grave, and the queries the narrator voices enhance and deepen the film.

we want guarantees, even warranties, on life itself. We resist — indeed resent — the notion that we are up against any limit, beginning with our natures, the central theme of Chapter Three.

The Christian tradition teaches us that we cannot transcend that which we are through our own unaided efforts. But, with Roy the replicant, we want to know and we want to escape our condition. Where did I come from? Where am I going? Peering into the future inevitably folds back to become a concern with the past, indeed with our origins. We know we cannot recapture that origin. But we also know that our evaluation of what is possible and desirable for human beings turns on a set of assumptions about who and what we are as creatures. Many contenders have offered accounts of our origins. We have Darwinian and paleontological offerings called scientific. Political theory presents states of nature, some more horrific than others (Hobbes springs readily to mind), whose only cure is a social contract. Jews and Christians share an account — the Genesis story — but how are we to interpret that account at present, to distill its meaning and its hold on us at this late date? This is by no means simple. We can, of course, simply abandon the creation story as so much archaic nonsense. But that is to abandon the ground of our own tradition and to deny that it yet offers us anything.

So let us look again. As an exercise in the theological, political, and ethical imagination, I am going to work through two competing interpretations that suggest rather different orientations to human nature and human possibility. The thinkers involved are two of the great Christian teachers of this century, both philosophical theologians, who emphasize or stress contrasting features of the narrative each shares. The names of these thinkers will be familiar to everyone: Dietrich Bonhoeffer and Karol Wojtyla, Pope John Paul II. Why them? Because their lives intersect with the searing events that have tortured and tormented our century — Nazism, Stalinism, World War II — and, for Pope John Paul II, continuing Soviet domination and a lingering Cold War followed by that extraordinary outbreak of hope and freedom marked by Solidarity in Poland, Civic Forum in Czechoslovakia, and other freedom movements leading up to the end of the Cold War. Bonhoeffer died a martyr for his anti-Nazism. Karol Wojtyla, studying for the priesthood underground, participating in illegal theatrical productions at the risk of his life, witnessed the reduction of his country to rubble, the killing of much of the Polish intelligentsia and priesthood (as high as 50 percent of priests in some regions of Poland), and the indescribable horrors of the Shoah set up by the Nazi aggressors on Polish land. Each, then, saw the worst. But each calls us to the best — to courage and to Christian hope. "Be not afraid!" were the first words of Karol Wojtyla's pontificate. Whatever a person's views on the positions taken or upheld by this extraordinary pope, all credit him with exceptional moral and physical courage. Bonhoeffer, as readers of this volume will know, might have lived out his life — all those years beckoning him — in safety on foreign shores, as a student and teacher at Union Theological Seminary in New York City, but he chose to return to the site of greatest danger and there he met his martyrdom. I have, then, consciously selected as exemplary figures two men who enacted the Christian life and witness in the most dangerous and deadly of circumstances — fighting totalitarianism. Given my own interest in political life and thought, this is reason enough. But there is more that should be noted.

Dietrich Bonhoeffer and Karol Wojtyla/John Paul II are forbiddingly complex writers who never shirk at tackling the most difficult questions. I realize that, at first glance, pairing up Bonhoeffer and Pope John Paul II in a consideration of the fall — the theme of this chapter — may seem to invite a foreordained conclusion that falls rather predictably along Lutheran/Catholic lines. But anyone familiar with the work of these two extraordinary figures will discern upon examination that things are by no means that simple. My first task, therefore, is to offer up an expository version of Bonhoeffer's and John Paul's accounts of creation and fall with textual commentary as I go. I will conclude with direct points of comparison and contrast that help to launch us into the subsequent discussions of what it means to forget that we are fallen.

What a treat it is to read Bonhoeffer and John Paul! This reading implicates us in the full weight of twentieth-century Western philosophy. Bonhoeffer worked his way through Nietzsche and Heidegger as well as the history of theology, primarily though not exclusively German. He was, as well, a generous and audacious reader of German literature — novels, poetry, drama. Readers of Bonhoeffer's *Letters and Papers from Prison* will recognize this characterization immediately, of course, given the sprinkling of requests for texts to be sent him that peppered Bonhoeffer's letters to his family. His *Creation and Fall* is a taut, closely argued exegetical study, and the references are largely internal to the scriptural text. By contrast, John Paul's catechesis on the book of Genesis affords a glimpse into his wide-ranging, complex encounter with philosophy generally, twentieth-century thought in particular. He references Lévy-Bruhl, Eliade, Tillich, Ricoeur, Levinas, Freud, Jung, dozens of Hebrew exegetical works, semioticians and etymologists, books in analytic philosophy and anthropology as well as classical Latin poets, Plato, Kant, Scheler, on and on. This in addition to the usual suspects — Augustine and Aquinas first and foremost.[2] We are not deal-

2. Those curious about John Paul's reading habits and impatient with slogging through his philosophical works, homilies, catechetical texts, and encyclicals might consult *Crossing the Threshold of Hope* for bibliographic hints. Although not referenced in his account of the fall, John Paul has worked through the corpus of works by Marx and, one has the impression, much of the major secondary work on Marx and Marxism.

ing with hermetically sealed-off, pious thinkers. These men were, and one still is, in the arena, embracing or challenging that whole complex of features and factors we call modernity.

LET'S BEGIN with Bonhoeffer, who is committed to the view that human beings are in rebellion against God. Who is this God? He is "wholly Creator, completely the Lord, and his creature remains totally the submissive, obedient creature, praising and worshipping him as the Lord. He [God] is never the creation. He is always the Creator. He is not the substance of nature; there is no continuum that binds or unites him with his work. There is only his *Word*."[3] God speaks and God is "never in the world in any way except in his absolute transcendence of it": this, for Bonhoeffer, is the God of Genesis 1. The portion of Genesis before the creation of man is a story, first, of remote-

3. Dietrich Bonhoeffer, *Creation and Fall,* trans. John C. Fletcher (New York: Macmillan, 1959), p. 22. Bonhoeffer's insistence on God's "otherness," namely, that God is *not* to be identified with his creation, is a powerful contrast to "Nazi Wholeness," as elaborated in Anne Harrington's superb book, *Reenchanted Science: Holism in German Culture from Wilhelm II to Hitler* (Princeton: Princeton University Press, 1996). The Nazi holistic approach was contrasted with the "Jewish international lie of scientific objectivity"; and, more importantly for my purposes, in Nazi "science" the part was seen as absorbed entirely within the whole and the whole was all there was. That is, the world was entirely, and holistically, made immanent, and a transcendent horizon (e.g., God's otherness) was eradicated and effaced. Within Nazi biopolitics, Jews represented a divisive, dissolutive principle; the *Volk,* the principle of wholeness. Bonhoeffer here anticipated any attempt to draw Christian theology into the orbit of *volkish* thinking. Indeed, certain Nazi scientific popularizers had attacked Christianity for its refusal to recognize that the "Volks-body is an organic whole" and for its attribution of "infinite worth" to each individual given his or her status as one of God's creatures (see especially Harrington, pp. 175-206).

ness.[4] Eternal, unchangeable laws come into being. This world is fixed — consider mathematical symbols that are identical even today in every culture and constitute perhaps the only transparent universal "language."

But then something new appears. The Creator wills that his creation "should affirm and continue his work, he wills that created things should live and create further life."[5] Vegetation springs up; the seas swarm; trees bear fruit; birds fly above the earth; creeping things begin their migration across the face of the earth. Bonhoeffer presents this as a kind of magical moment. Then we get to man. God creates man in his own image: "male and female created he them" (Gen. 1:27). Bonhoeffer does not make too much of the *them* at this point — the plural that suggests a simultaneity in creation of male/female that the textually later but chronologically earlier Yahwist account (Gen. 2:24) undermines with its fashioning of Eve from Adam's rib. For Bonhoeffer, the plural in Hebrew is a way of "showing the significance and sublimity of the Creator's action."[6] Man (and Bonhoeffer's language does not limit his exposition to the male) is the "new, free, undetermined work of God."[7] But, as we shall see, his exegesis requires that Adam precede Eve in time, if not in ontological equality and dignity.

A great divide separates us from this point of origin. We cannot leap back "into the world of lost beginning. It is hopeless to want to know for ourselves what man was originally, to identify here man's ideal with the creational reality of God, not to understand that we can know about the man of the beginning only if we start from Christ."[8] This new being, this free man, is not free

4. "Man" is meant as the male person here, as Bonhoeffer, unlike John Paul, privileges the Yahwist (Gen. 2:24) account.

5. *Creation and Fall*, p. 33.

6. *Creation and Fall*, p. 36.

7. *Creation and Fall*, p. 36.

8. *Creation and Fall*, p. 37.

as such. "Freedom is not a quality of man, nor is it an ability . . . freedom is not a quality which can be revealed — it is not a possession, a presence, an object, nor is it a form of existence — but a relationship and nothing else. In truth, freedom is a relationship between two persons. Being free means 'being free for the other,' because the other has bound me to him. In relationship with the other am I free. No substantial or individualistic concept of freedom can conceive of freedom."[9] Here Bonhoeffer strikes one of his key themes, namely, that the individual exists only for "the other." Insofar as the person is a concrete "I," the other must be a concrete "Thou."

This relationship in freedom is something hard won after the fall, as we shall learn. But at the moment of "created he them," man is dependent on another, and it is "in this dependence on the other that his creatureliness consists."[10] Man and woman are for Bonhoeffer "man in duality" given dominion from God over God's creation. Man belongs to the world completely in and through the relational recognition that gives him dominion over that which nourishes and sustains him. In his freedom he is bound. Bonhoeffer does not make much of the male/female aspect of "them" at this point save to speak of dependence on God and on the rest of creation even as man in his "duality" is *primus inter pares* among created beings. Consider the themes thus far: freedom is a relationship, and our creatureliness consists in the dependence that is the ground of our freedom.[11]

Moving to the second account of human creation in Genesis

9. *Creation and Fall,* p. 37.
10. *Creation and Fall,* p. 38.
11. Cf. Martin Luther, "The Freedom of a Christian," in Timothy F. Lull, ed., *Martin Luther's Basic Theological Writings* (Minneapolis: Fortress Press, 1989), pp. 585-629: "We conclude, therefore, that a Christian lives not in himself, but in Christ and in his neighbor. Otherwise he is not a Christian" (p. 623).

MEDIA LIBRARY
WOODMONT BAPTIST CHURCH
2100 WOODMONT BLVD.
NASHVILLE, TN 37215

2:24, Bonhoeffer notes that "everything takes place in a very earthly way. The language is extremely childlike, and shocking for those to want to 'understand,' to know anything."[12] We moderns are likely to find the anthropomorphisms "intolerable": forming and shaping clay; breathing life into dust and the like. Darwin and Feuerbach "could not speak any more strongly. Man's origin is in a piece of earth."[13] We do not *have* a body. We simply *are* body and soul, ensouled bodies.[14] "Man in the beginning is really his body." And this human existence binds the creature to "mother earth." Man — and apparently Bonhoeffer construes man as singular, not plural at this point — is "naked and unashamed." He "speaks and walks with God."[15] These are "ancient, magical," yet powerful pictures. But something stands in the middle of the garden — the tree of knowledge of good and evil. Adam does not know what death is, what good and evil are; he does not know a limit, living as he does in unbroken obedience. His creatureliness marks a limit but he does not yet know this. God, to be sure, tries to convey it by forbidding eating of the tree. But Adam, in freedom, does not acknowledge that the limit lies at the heart — the middle — of existence, not on the extreme, not at some periphery. "Adam knows neither what is good nor what is evil; in the most particular sense he lives beyond good and evil, beyond *tob* and *ra*."[16]

I cannot here resist a sidebar comment, namely, that by locating "beyond good and evil" in a prelapsarian realm we can nei-

---

12. *Creation and Fall*, p. 46.

13. *Creation and Fall*, p. 46.

14. This becomes critical later as we consider just how gnostic is the current moment. Our bodies are nuisances and inconveniences, if not outright sources of pollution. We like to think we are souls — intelligences — who just happen to have bodies.

15. *Creation and Fall*, p. 49.

16. *Creation and Fall*, p. 53.

ther recapture nor reclaim, Bonhoeffer is surely taking a sturdy swipe at Nietzsche. To seek to move beyond good and evil once the point of origin is lost is to stake out far too much territory for oneself — for the creature — and against the Creator. For *tob* and *ra* — good and evil — "are the categories for the deepest division of human life in every aspect."[17] Man as *sicut deus* — the "creator-man" — through the fall cannot recreate himself as man before the fall. For he now *knows* good and evil, and he cannot pretend that he is unaware of this knowledge. Even with the "utmost endeavor of our imagination and all the other powers of our souls," human beings "are simply not in a position to remove ourselves to this paradise 'beyond good and evil.' "[18] Back to the main story.

Adam is alone.[19] Adam finds no real companion among the animals. He loves them as brothers but they are "strange." Eve, there when Adam awakens from his deep sleep, is unique. He feels gratitude. He is "connected in a completely new way to this Eve, who derives her existence from him."[20] They are two, yet one; one, yet two. This other person "derives from" yet "limits" Adam in the form of a "bodily representation" as the "limit placed upon me by God." It is unclear at this juncture from what point of view Bonhoeffer is speaking. Can Adam recognize Eve

17. *Creation and Fall,* p. 54.

18. *Creation and Fall,* p. 57.

19. Bonhoeffer makes an interesting move here by comparing Adam in his aloneness to Christ, who was also alone. But then, so are we all, he concludes, each in our own way. Christ is alone "because he loves the other person, because he is the way by which mankind has returned to its Creator. We are alone because we have pushed the other person from us, because we hated him. Adam was alone in hope, Christ was alone in the fullness of deity, and we are alone in evil, in hopelessness" (*Creation and Fall,* p. 59). Denial of relationality and dependence is a terrible aloneness: we have pushed the other person from us.

20. *Creation and Fall,* p. 60.

as presenting a "limit" when he does not yet have knowledge of good and evil? Man remains naked and unashamed. This surely means that the limit Bonhoeffer here adumbrates is "objective," an evaluation deriving from the account itself rather than from what was epistemologically available to Adam at that juncture. In other words, the word *objective,* that which is simply given, part of the order of things, does not require a moment of recognition to exist. Bonhoeffer is here outside the account, so to speak, noting an objective limit yet to be recognized by Adam.

If man hates his limit, it destroys community; if he only "wants to possess or deny the other person without limit," he has placed himself in a Hegelian master/slave dialectic rather than in a different sort of narrative wherein the loving recognition of the other cannot be used to underwrite a struggle unto death.[21] The other person is a helper, and the grace of this helper helps us to bear our limit and to live before God.[22] If we deny the other person, what we should have "received humbly now becomes the occasion for glorification and revolt."[23] Sexuality, becoming one flesh, is our realization of belonging to another. We are not yet ashamed, for shame exists "as a result of the knowledge of the division of man, of the division of the world in general. . . . Shame is the expression of the fact that we no longer accept the other person as the gift of God."[24] So: knowledge, death, sexuality, these three "primaeval words of life" come into existence in a

21. This loving recognition is not compatible, as I have indicated, with a master/slave narrative. But it can comport with relationships of sovereign/ subject or ruler/ruled — not my main concern at this juncture.

22. Cf. Luther, "Freedom of a Christian," who argues that "from faith thus flow forth love and joy in the Lord, and from love a joyful, willing, and free mind that serves one's neighbor willingly and takes no account of gratitude or ingratitude, of praise or blame, of gain or loss . . . love . . . makes us free, joyful . . . servants of our neighbors, and yet lords of all" (p. 619).

23. *Creation and Fall,* p. 61.

24. *Creation and Fall,* p. 63.

world of division. To pretend at that juncture — at *our* juncture — that we are prelapsarians is, for Bonhoeffer, arrogant madness.

For when we fell, it was a long, hard fall indeed. Woman becomes a seducer. The serpent, one of God's creatures, becomes an instrument of evil. But the Bible is not concerned to cast aspersions, Bonhoeffer argues. We cannot reproduce the moment. We can, however, say that God's truth points to a limit, while the serpent's truth points to limitlessness — that we might have knowledge as unto God's — and that both of these enter into the post-fall *imago dei,* or our understanding of what it means to be created in God's image. *Imago dei* — "the creature living in the unity of obedience; *sicut deus* — the creature living out of the division of good and evil."[25] It is not until the Incarnation that the image of God is fully restored, according to Bonhoeffer (not until *agnus dei* — the One who was sacrificed).

The fall "*really* makes a creator, the *sicut deus* man, out of the creature, the *imago dei* man."[26] Eve falls first as the weaker. But the culmination is the fall of Adam; indeed, "Eve only falls totally when Adam falls, for the two are one. Adam falls because of Eve, Eve falls because of Adam, the two are one. In their guilt too they are two and yet one. They fall together as one and each one carries all the guilt alone. Male and female he created them — and man fell away from him — male and female."[27] Interestingly, Bonhoeffer returns to the textually first but chronologically later, or Elohist, account of creation at this juncture in the form of a partial indictment. Created he them and *they* are responsible for the fall; they are together in guilt. This defection is dire, described by Bonhoeffer as a "continual falling, a plunging into

25. *Creation and Fall,* p. 71.
26. *Creation and Fall,* p. 73.
27. *Creation and Fall,* p. 75.

bottomless depths, a being relinquished, a withdrawal even farther and deeper. And in all this it is not simply a moral lapse but the destruction of creation by the creature."[28] Bonhoeffer tells us that he is not very interested in why evil exists: that is not, for him, a "theological question, for it assumes that it is possible to go beyond the existence forced upon us by sinners." No, the theological question does not arise here but only with "the real overcoming of evil on the Cross; it asks for forgiveness of guilt, for the reconciliation of the fallen world."[29]

Post-fall we are in a world of troubles. Man and woman are divided. Sexuality transgresses limits in "avid passion of man for the other person. . . . Sexuality is the passionate hatred of every limit, it is arbitrariness to the highest degree, it is self-will, it is avid, impotent will for unity in the divided world. . . . Sexuality desires the destruction of the other person as creature. . . . Man without a limit, hating, avidly passionate, does not show himself in his nakedness."[30] Covering himself assures that the world is rent and torn into *tob* and *ra*. Henceforth man lives in a "peculiar dialectic," hating the limit, as one divided. Shame, or covering and concealment, and the vocation of the "restrained community of marriage in the Church" alone structure restraint. Man's creatureliness is now corrupted. No wonder man is ashamed. The tree of knowledge brought on Adam and Eve "shame and passion." Shame requires that we wear a mask. But from beneath "the mask there is the longing for the restoration of the lost unity." This forces its way toward fulfillment in the partnership of two human beings in marriage; shame, at that point, reveals its "deepest secrecy," the yearning for a world without the need for shame.[31]

28. *Creation and Fall,* p. 76.
29. *Creation and Fall,* p. 76.
30. *Creation and Fall,* p. 84.
31. These passages are drawn from Bonhoeffer's *Ethics,* trans. Neville Horton Smith (New York: Simon and Schuster, 1995), p. 25.

Eve, fallen, is nonetheless "the mother of all living," or is called such by Adam from a stance of "wild exultation, defiance, insolence, and victory." Eve is our first and sullied beginning. Mary, "the innocent, unknowing mother of God — this is the second beginning."[32] The earth awaits Mary's motherhood and Christ's incarnation. It all gets worse before anything better is intimated. Cain and murder are yet to come. But Christ on the cross is the "end of the story of Cain," and the cross on Golgotha offers us a "strange paradise . . . this blood, this broken body! What a strange tree of life, this tree on which God himself must suffer and die. . . . The tree of life, the Cross of Christ, the middle of the fallen and preserved world of God, for us that is the end of the story of paradise."[33] Humans can achieve nothing by their own efforts. The cross and God's free gift of grace alone redeem us: here Bonhoeffer calls to mind Luther's "On the Bondage of the Will," perhaps the most bleak of Luther's assessments of our fallen condition. Only this abyss, this utter forlornness, helps us to recognize by contrast the unwarranted bounty of God's free gift of grace. Our hope and yearning must be marked by the sign of the cross lest we fall into the arrogant presumption that we are meritorious. With Luther, it is the whole person who falls and the whole person who must be redeemed: "If we believe that Christ has redeemed men by his blood, we are bound to confess that the whole man was lost; otherwise, we should make Christ either superfluous or the redeemer of only the lowest part of man, which would be blasphemy and sacrilege."[34] If the Bonhoeffer/Luther account offers a low anthropology — do not expect too much from creatures who have fallen so far — there is

32. *Creation and Fall,* p. 87.
33. *Creation and Fall,* pp. 93-94.
34. "On the Bondage of the Will," in Lull, ed., *Martin Luther's Basic Theological Writings,* pp. 173-226 (in excerpt), quotation from p. 224.

joyous anticipation in the high Christology. Relinquishment and redemption are twins, not opposites.

IT IS John Paul II's turn to lead us into and out of the Garden. The gravamen of John Paul's narrative is very different from that of Bonhoeffer. Bonhoeffer, remember, is at pains to occlude the point of origin or, perhaps better put, to teach us that that point forever eludes us and is not, in any case, interesting theologically. The fall inaugurates the story that really interests Bonhoeffer. John Paul, however, is far more engaged with "from the beginning," with the sorts of creatures we were and have remained given that beginning. He knows, of course, that we cannot penetrate to the beginning in a historical sense, but he argues that we can offer intimations in an anthropological sense. Thus, in Jesus' exchange with the Pharisees in Matthew 19:3ff., Jesus recalls the ancient truth: "Have you not read that he who made them from the beginning made them male and female?"[35] John Paul segues from this moment to the "beginning" Jesus has in mind, namely, Genesis 1:27, "In the beginning the Creator made them male and female." This passage means not only that God created "them" in his image but also that God did so "in the beginning." So Jesus himself lifts up the Elohist account.

What sorts of creatures were these? First and foremost, they are creatures created for communion, to be in *communio*. But there is that second account of creation, from Genesis 2:24, an account that, according to John Paul, "forms a conceptual and stylistic unity with the description of original innocence, man's

35. The discussion that follows is drawn from John Paul II, *Original Unity of Man and Woman: Catechesis on the Book of Genesis* (Boston: St. Paul Editions, 1981). All references unless otherwise noted are from this collected series of General Audience presentations by the Holy Father in his weekly audiences from September 5, 1979, to April 2, 1980.

happiness, and also his first fall." Then John Paul kicks into italics in the text with these words: *"From the point of view of biblical criticism,* it is necessary to mention immediately that *the first account of man's creation is chronologically* later than the second. The origin of this latter is much more remote. This more ancient text is defined as 'Yahwist' because the term 'Yahweh' is used to denominate God."[36] By comparison with this second but earlier account, the first and chronologically later "is much more mature both as regards the image of God, and as regards the formulation of the essential truths about man. This account derives from the priestly and 'elohist' tradition, from 'Elohim,' the term used in that account for God."[37] Very interesting, some might murmur, but what is the import of this? John Paul gets straight to the point. The textually earlier but chronologically later account is clear that man is "male and female" — always was, always will be. The ontological equality and essential relationality of male and female is given as a corporeal reality. This is the "essential truth" — male and female created he them. This account, according to John Paul, is "free from any trace whatsoever of subjectivism. It contains only the objective facts and defines the objective reality, both when it speaks of man's creation, male and female, in the image of God, and when it adds a little later the words of the first blessing: 'Be fruitful and multiply, and fill the earth; subdue it and have dominion over it'" (Gen. 1:28).[38]

This leads John Paul directly into the heart of his theology of the body. He turns next to the "subjective definition of man" he finds embedded in the second account (Gen. 2:24). John Paul makes much of these two distinct accounts; Bonhoeffer blurs them and discusses them interchangeably at points. But John

36. *Catechesis*, p. 21.
37. *Catechesis*, p. 22.
38. *Catechesis*, p. 23.

Paul clearly wants to put the heavy theological, philosophical, and anthropological weight on Genesis 1:27 — "created he them." So how does he deal with Genesis 2:24? He speaks rather like a cultural and philosophical anthropologist. "The second chapter of Genesis constitutes, in a certain manner, the most ancient description and record of man's self-knowledge."[39] The narrative is archaic, manifesting a primitive mythical character. Its various elements have become clearer to us given the work of contemporary philosophical anthropology. Thus it "could be said that Genesis 2 presents the creation of man especially in its subjective aspect."[40] The pope brings a bit of his etymological armamentarium to bear at this point, telling us that "the first human being the Bible calls 'Man *(adam)*" but very briefly. For "from the moment of the creation of the first woman, it begins to call him 'man' *(ish),* in relation to *ishshah* ('woman')."[41]

Thus we find two human persons, *ish* and *ishshah,* in the Garden. And there is that mysterious tree. This tree of the knowledge of good and evil "is the line of demarcation between the two original situations of which the Book of Genesis speaks." Here too there is a significant difference from Bonhoeffer, who locates the tree not at any boundary or liminal divide but at the very center. Bonhoeffer's Garden of Eden foreshadows his *theologia crucis,* so to speak. John Paul's Adam is innocent in a not terribly interesting way, a kind of naif. Indeed, the first situation is one of original innocence — innocent because "man (male and female) is, as it were, outside the sphere of knowledge of good and evil." But the second situation is fast upon us in which man (male and female), "after having disobeyed the Creator's command . . . finds himself, in a certain way, within the

39. *Catechesis,* p. 28.
40. *Catechesis,* p. 28.
41. *Catechesis,* p. 29.

sphere of the knowledge of good and evil. This second situation determines the state of human sinfulness, in contrast to the state of primitive innocence."[42] John Paul concludes that the Yahwist text shows that there are "two original situations," and "systematic theology" must "discern in these two antithetical situations two different states of human nature: the state of integral nature and the state of fallen nature." After the fall, we can no longer "read" signs correctly, so to speak, for a rupture has been effected between reality and our capacity to know that reality through the use of signs. We can only read signs correctly if we understand the realities to which these signs refer. But our ability to do this is deeply disturbed post-fall. So a fully integral nature must elude us.

But we live in expectation.

All of this is of fundamental significance "for the theology of the body." There are normative conclusions "which have an essential significance not only for ethics, but especially for the theology of man and for the theology of the body." This theology of the body is constituted on the basis of the Word of God: hence the importance of the Genesis accounts.[43] We fall, yes, but it is remarkable in what measured tones — in terms of rue and regret rather than catastrophe — John Paul addresses the fall. He sees the fall not so much as a horrific debacle, a shift to man as avid, a destroyer; rather, he represents it as a kind of brokenness, a rending of the seamless garment. Man breaks the original covenant with God in his and her heart. This serves to delimit two "diametrically opposed situations and states: that of original innocence and that of original sin." What we fall into is history. With Paul Ricoeur, John Paul suggests that the ontological and the historical here part company. When Christ refers to the begin-

42. *Catechesis,* p. 30.
43. *Catechesis,* p. 31.

ning in Matthew 19:3, he helps us *"to find in man an essential continuity and a link* between these two different states or dimensions of the human being." We are torn creatures but not utterly debased. And it is "impossible to understand the state of 'historical' sinfulness, without referring or appealing . . . to the state of original 'prehistoric' and fundamental innocence." For John Paul there is something like a fading from the fullness of the *imago dei* available to male/female once the historical threshold is crossed. Human rootedness in "revealed theological prehistory" is such that at every point our historical sinfulness can be explained only with reference to original innocence. "If this sin signifies, in every historical man, a state of lost grace, then it also contains a reference to that grace, which was precisely the grace of original innocence."[44] One might say that an ontological trace remains, grazing the brow and palpating the heart however gently of historically sinful man — male and female. The fall is a boundary experience that does not permit us direct contact with what lies on the other side, but does point us to it and draws us as close to it as possible — given certain forms of recognition and belief and the workings of grace.

What is human existence in history, after the fall, or perhaps the slide into sin (with an act of disobedience), for John Paul? After breaking the original covenant with the Creator, the promise of redemption is proffered early on, in the "so-called Proto-gospel in Genesis 3:15," and from that moment the creature *"begins to live in the theological perspective of the redemption,"* a redemption in which the human being participates as a historical being. Our participation is double: as part of the history of human sinfulness and as part of the history of salvation. We are both subjects and co-creators of that history.[45] From the perspective of "the redemption

44. *Catechesis,* p. 37.
45. *Catechesis,* p. 38.

of the body" continuity is guaranteed "between the hereditary state of man's sin and his original innocence, although this innocence was, historically, lost by him irremediably."[46]

Matters grow ever more complex as John Paul proceeds. We sense that he has rather different fish to fry from Bonhoeffer's. Concerned less with the depths of our sinfulness than Bonhoeffer (or, for that matter, Luther), John Paul lifts up God's desire that we move out of solitude and into communion: "It is not good that man should be alone." Before God, created "man finds himself . . . in search of his own entity: it could be said: in search of the definition of himself. A contemporary would say: in search of his own 'identity.'" The person alone cannot find himself or herself. And this man, John Paul insists, is "solitary without reference to sex."[47] The Genesis account makes this clear, he asserts. Solitariness is our human condition as human beings alone. Our self-awareness is at once an achievement and a gift. We are able to discern between "good and evil, between life and death."[48] A central problem of anthropology — consciousness of the body — is here touched on. Self-awareness becomes a requirement, so to speak, once the historic divide between solitude and innocence, recognition of the other and brokenness, is effected.

The heart and soul of the anthropological matter for John Paul is the original unity of man and woman. Male and female are two ways of "being a body."[49] John Paul makes a very interesting move in his discussion of Adam's deep sleep that occasions fashioning Eve from his rib. Because, for John Paul, we already

---

46. *Catechesis,* p. 39.

47. One wishes that the Vatican translators would try to use language in English that signifies what John Paul means to signify, in this text and many others, namely, that "man" in Polish — the language in which he writes the encyclicals — is not limited to the male, rather like the German "Mensch."

48. *Catechesis,* p. 51.

49. *Catechesis,* p. 62.

are male and female before Adam's deep sleep, what are we to make of Adam's recognition of Eve upon awakening? For John Paul, this does not signify that an entity that was not there before suddenly appears before Adam but, rather, that Adam falls into the sleep akin to nonbeing and awakens to recognize the double unity of male and female, a recognition all of us must make. "The rib" John Paul treats as an "archaic, metaphorical and figurative way" of expressing the thought of homogeneity of somatic structure: "bone of my bones, flesh of my flesh." Thus: "Somatic homogeneity, in spite of the difference in constitution bound up with the sexual difference, is so evident that the man (male), on waking up from the genetic sleep, expresses it at once."[50] The Hebrew term *adam* captures this "collective concept of the human species" in the way many modern Indo-European languages do not, claims John Paul.

The significance of all this lies in the fact that it is the *communion* of persons *(communio personarum)* that is the authentic reflection of the *imago dei* — not man (male or female) alone. Communion expresses more than help or a helper; it names the existence of the person *for* another, of the gift of the self to another. It is a special reciprocity; it affords intimations of an inscrutable divine communion. "Man [male and female] becomes the image of God not so much in the moment of solitude as in the moment of communion."[51] This second narrative, then, serves as a preparation for "understanding . . . the Trinitarian concept of the 'image of God. . . .' We have arrived at the core of anthropological reality, the name of which is 'body,' the human body. This body 'right from the beginning' is bound up 'in the image of God.'"[52] What are we to make of such primordial hu-

50. *Catechesis,* p. 66.
51. *Catechesis,* pp. 63-64.
52. *Catechesis,* p. 75.

man experiences as shame? The human, having fallen into history, cannot consciously perceive his or her lost ontological "self," but, in a certain sense, our self-awareness "presupposes" that beginning.[53] Originally, we were not ashamed. This shameless or shame-free experience of the body is now lost to us. All of human history is colored by such "fundamental experiences . . . as the experience of shame."[54] Shame is a new situation. We failed the test connected with the tree of knowledge of good and evil. Shame is a marker, a "boundary" experience. This cuts much deeper than the sense of sight — first "seeing," then feeling shame. It is an experience of anxiety regarding one's second self (male or female) unknown in the state of original innocence, also, remember, a state of nonrecognition. Shame is deeply "rooted . . . in mutual relations," and it expresses "the essential rules for the 'communion of persons' in history."[55] We lost the capacity for full communication, to be fully in communion as body-subjects. We communicate and we see (through a glass darkly, one might interject, though John Paul does not) and what we see is not just an "exterior" perception but an "interior dimension of participation in the vision of the Creator."[56] Still, it is only through reciprocity — through processes of mutual recognition — that we come to know the meaning of our own bodies. It is only through the gift of the self that we come to understand communion. (John Paul calls this "the hermeneutics of the gift.")

The remainder of John Paul's account is devoted to the way the body-subject is a gift from a loving Creator to a creature who can, in turn, make a gift of him- or herself to others. We make ourselves a gift in the freedom of love "from the beginning." In

53. *Catechesis,* p. 86.
54. *Catechesis,* p. 88.
55. *Catechesis,* p. 93.
56. *Catechesis,* p. 99.

this beginning there is "the freedom of the gift in the human body. It means that this body possesses a full 'nuptial' meaning." Men and women's mutual experience of the body involves a real communion of persons. Each, in giving, is enriched. Each grows "by virtue of the interior disposition to the exchange of the gift and to the extent to which it means with the same and even deeper acceptance and welcome, as the fruit of a more and more intense awareness of the gift itself."[57]

How is any or all of this possible post-fall and in history? It is something that must be reconstructed "with great effort, the meaning of the disinterested mutual gift." John Paul has no doubt that this is in fact possible. To the skeptic, he says, "following the trail of the 'historical *a posteriori*' — and above all, following the trail of human hearts — we can reproduce and, as it were, reconstruct that mutual exchange of the gift of the person, which was described in the ancient text, so rich and deep, of the Book of Genesis."[58] We all bear within ourselves the trace of our beginning. We cannot know it, not fully, but we can "with great effort," in history, reconstruct it in a real if imperfect way.

IT IS now the moment to draw these two accounts together in order to draw out points of difference and of commonality that will offer conceptual and framing reference points for the chapters to follow.

First, Bonhoeffer and John Paul are working with rather different images of God. Bonhoeffer's is very much the post-Occam God as the site of sovereign will, a remote Creator who comes close to us only through the Incarnation and the cross. God incarnate, the second person of the Trinity, is the heart of the mat-

57. *Catechesis,* p. 164.
58. *Catechesis,* p. 132.

ter. For John Paul, God is not so much the site of monistic will as a representation of the fullness of understanding, reason, the plenitude of power and Being itself. Does this mean human beings within Bonhoeffer's treatment *need* the cross more than John Paul's body-subjects do? This would be unnecessarily provocative, as John Paul, too, emphasizes Jesus as the very heart of what we mean by "the gift," the way in which God's transcendent divinity breaks into immanence without losing the grandeur of the transcendent. For Bonhoeffer, as for Luther, we throw ourselves upon the cross. For John Paul, we live in expectation of Christ. "If it is true that man of himself, despite his good will, cannot achieve salvation, the one who seriously and alertly faces his human experience finally discovers within himself the 'urgent need for an encounter' which is marvellously satisfied by Christ."[59] The most important point for our subsequent discussion is that neither Bonhoeffer's more mordant reading of our condition nor John Paul's more optimistic account presents us as in any way self-sovereign. Although our reasoning capacity is more intact for John Paul, it is deeply flawed and imperfect. Original sin has not completely "ruined us," as Luther alleges in his most dire musings, but we certainly cannot, through our own effort, reconstitute ourselves as whole.

Second, John Paul places greater emphasis on "created he them" than does Bonhoeffer. This is central to John Paul's integral anthropology. There is more fleshing out of an explicit anthropology in John Paul's discussion. And the creature who emerges is credited with greater powers of discernment than Bonhoeffer affords his early creatures. John Paul's humans are always "man alone" *as a double* (i.e., as male and female); for Bonhoeffer, Adam is *really alone* before the creation of Eve in

59. Pope John Paul II, *Daily Meditations* (Sherbrooke, Quebec: Editions Paulines, 1984), p. 9.

Genesis 2. Does anything important turn on this? There is certainly a different placing of accent. As well, John Paul's anthropology puts greater pressure on any and all comparisons between men and women that treat gender differences as invidious or as the occasion for unjustifiable discrimination. John Paul never speaks of Eve as a seducer, for example.

Third, the divide that separates humans pre- and postlapsarian is wider for Bonhoeffer than for John Paul. As well, Bonhoeffer places greater stress on our disobedience and our sinfulness, our avid destructiveness. For John Paul the fall seems not so much a plunging over a cliff as a slide into the Slough of Despond. We are stuck but the divide is not as great. This is linked to where each places the tree of the knowledge of good and evil: for Bonhoeffer at the very center; for John Paul at a liminal boundary, an edge.

Fourth, communion and being *in communio* are given greater weight in John Paul's treatment than in Bonhoeffer's, particularly in the notion of the nuptial gift relationship. We are yearning creatures marked by the trace of our lost communion. The gift of each to the other in marriage bears witness to this. For Bonhoeffer, marriage is required by the sin that is sexuality after the fall. John Paul goes much further in redeeming sexual relationships. This also carries implications for their respective accounts of shame — for Bonhoeffer as a limit that marks our sinfulness; for John Paul as a call to self-consciousness.

Fifth, each weighs in powerfully against any and all individualistic and strongly voluntaristic construals of human life and freedom. Each utterly opposes any notion of a sovereign, wholly autonomous self. Bonhoeffer would join John Paul in being appalled at contemporary, radical appeals to autarky, self-sufficiency, and self-possession. They join hands in a countercultural struggle against the idols of the present moment.

Finally, there is Eve and there is Mary. Bonhoeffer harshly

32

criticizes Adam's presumption in naming Eve "the mother of all." Eve is fallen and it is not until Mary, whose motherhood is innocent and unknowing (in the sexual sense), that our human inheritance is reconciled and redeemed. Her maternity prefigures the cross. John Paul treats Eve differently. He puts Eve and Mary on a continuum rather than driving a wedge between them, describing Mary as "the second Eve." For the first woman, after all, acknowledges that she has "gotten a man with the help of the Lord" (Gen. 4:1). This shows Eve is fully aware "of the mystery of creation, which is renewed in human generation. She is also fully aware of the creative participation that God has in human generation."[60] These first parents "transmit to all human parents — even after sin, together with the fruit of the tree of knowledge of good and evil and almost at the threshold of all 'historical' experiences — the fundamental truth about the birth of man in the image of God, according to natural laws."[61] There

---

60. *Catechesis,* pp. 157-58. Given all the many and various ways that the "cult of Mary" plays itself out, and in light of Protestant hostility toward any such "cult," it might be worth noting what theological moment lay behind the emergence of the cult of Mary in the first instance. It was at the Council of Ephesus that Mary was designated *Theotokos,* "God-bearer," which becomes, in Latin, *Mater dei,* "Mother of God." "Mary was not a pipe through which divine spirit inserted itself into earthly matter, or a bag in which the precious spice of the Godhead was temporarily contained, but the intimate source of the human identity of God himself, giving to God incarnate all that a mother gives to her children — blood, bone, nerve and personality. In her conceiving and childbearing heaven and earth were wedded beyond any possibility of divorce: a stupendous miracle had occurred which raised human nature to heaven itself" (Eamon Duffy, "True and False Madonnas," *The Tablet* [6 February 1999]: 169-171; quotation, p. 169). Duffy rejects the "hortatory and moralistic" uses of the Marian tradition, embracing instead, as he argues that the church did at Vatican II, Marian devotion as a way to explore "the beauty and tenderness of the Incarnation" (p. 170). It is this dimension John Paul surely evokes.

61. *Catechesis,* p. 158.

is, in John Paul's story, an image of continuity and unity that Bonhoeffer ruptures.

But each stresses the centrality of our need to be at God's disposal; each celebrates the gift of life and of grace; each insists that we are human insofar as we are in relationship and for the other. This means that each is somewhat opaque to us in late modernity, for we no longer understand the meaning of the donative gift, of putting ourselves at the disposal of another. The gift economy that Bonhoeffer and John Paul embrace, each in his own way, has long since been replaced by a consumer economy that sees us as most human when we are most fully in possession of our self and anything else we can lay our hands on. Perhaps we have fallen further than Bonhoeffer believed we could — although probably not considering the time and place in which he wrote — but certainly further than John Paul believes we should, given the high hopes he holds forth for love and for reason. That is why, on a highly speculative note, I believe John Paul is, if anything, far more brokenhearted about human sinfulness than was Bonhoeffer, who believed that the beasts were always straining at their leashes, rattling their chains, and awaiting release upon a complacent and uncomprehending and perhaps even occasionally joyous world.[62] And we are the beasts.

Unfortunately, there are only too many "signs of the times," as John Paul calls them, that would seem to bear Bonhoeffer out. I turn next to instances of what it means to forget that we are fallen. As I do so, I weave back and forth between the presuppositions that undergird Bonhoeffer's and John Paul's accounts, re-

62. It was only in reading the galleys for this book that I was hit by a moment of recognition, namely, that I had here fashioned a version of the sentence with which Albert Camus ends his novel *The Plague.* The sentence is long and refers to the plague bacillus that never dies and may "rouse up its rats again and send them forth to die in a happy city" (*The Plague* [New York: Vintage Books, 1972], p. 287).

spectively. For they are part of our shared Christian tradition. If my own formation was in and through that great document, Luther's *Small Catechism,* much of my adult thinking has been shaped by a reading of Catholic theology and social thought. It is unsurprising, therefore, that I have begun with great teachers of these mutually enriching strands in our tradition. The themes that Bonhoeffer and John Paul leave us offer rich theological anthropologies, with each treating the body in relation to shame, knowledge of good and evil, and finitude. We are also left with difficult challenges concerning the scope of human agency, willing, and willfulness and we are deeded quandaries concerning just how far removed from us is prelapsarian nature. Is it an incommensurable divide, one no human knowledge, understanding, and yearning can approach? Or can we derive some knowledge of that for which we long and of which we yet bear a trace? Two of the arenas of human existence in the *saeculum,* in the time between creation and the eschaton, that plunge us deep into all these questions are those forms of human self-creation and fashioning we know as economics and technological and scientific change that takes as its experimental epicenter the human body itself. Unsurprisingly, these are endeavors that provide ample scope for human creativity but also for human action and willing that unleashes our desire to dominate and to master, that, indeed, turns on the lust to dominate in the first instance. The temptations are many; the sins among the "deadly." I refer to *pride* and *sloth.* We turn, first, to economics and the sin of pride.

THE FORCE OF INTENT

At times we force our destiny like rivers
carving canyons to the sea or trees
that crack the rocks they wedge to reach the light.

But the politics of will depend on change,
the force of our intent in circumstance.
How easily we trample the green havens,

dissolve chapels of mist in scorching light.
How quickly we bridle at roadblocks and chasms
and turn from the philosophy of lakes.

But our certainties are destined for revision
like morning maps of an evening land. We know
at last the mountains are more than we supposed,

and our wagons sit stranded by snow in the pass.
The yellow pride of noon turns blue at dusk.
The walking boy becomes the wheelchair man.

FRED DINGS,
from *Eulogy for a Private Man*
(reprinted with permission of the author)

Chapter Two

Forgetting That We Are Fallen:
The Prideful Self

What can we expect from fallen creatures? Whether emerging from the dire account of the fall offered by Bonhoeffer (and, before him, by Luther and Calvin) or the less catastrophic position embodied in John Paul II's catechesis on Genesis, one can reasonably anticipate from such creatures a good measure of pridefulness that includes, or is premised in the first instance on, forgetfulness that one is, in fact, a *creature,* begotten and interdependent. Our sociality goes all the way through and down. Our indebtednesses are beyond measure. Yet, at present, pride is scarcely thought of as a sin; if anything, it is a call to arms. Self-overcoming is one way to depict how we, as a people, do the things we do and unstoppably aim for more, better, bigger, faster, newer in this hard-driven culture of ours. We believe that our desires should have nigh uninhibited freedom to operate even as we ourselves move about as required as life takes on a more temporary, less sturdy and stable, quality.

Advertising plays to the self consumed by consumption. A recent advertisement for Camry Solara pitches the automobile to adults (there is a woman, back turned, featured in the ad) but to adults who are, at base, little kids. The copy reads, in full: "Little Kids Are Selfish. Impulsive. They Don't Make Rational Decisions. When They See Something They Want, They Want It Now. Little Kids Have a Lot of Fun. Hmmmm." We want it and we want it now. But nothing lasts. So we will need more and very soon at that. In a recent work, the historian William Leach finds himself reflecting on what he calls "the destruction of place in American life."[1] Our lives are increasingly formed — or kept permanently formless — within the swirling vortex of temporariness: temporary homes, jobs, vehicles, schools, mates. "A vast landscape of the temporary has arisen, peopled with thousands of floating executives and countless numbers of part-time and temporary workers, all unable or unwilling to make long-term connections to their communities. A service economy, whose key industries are tourism and gambling, has grown up to threaten the settled character of towns, cities, and regions. A system of great research universities also belongs to this universe, fostering transnational mobility and a disposition to think and live beyond America."[2]

1. William Leach, *A Country of Exiles: The Destruction of Place in American Life* (New York: Pantheon, 1999).

2. Leach, *Country of Exiles,* p. 6. As I revise this chapter, I am sitting in the "dining area" of very temporary housing of the sort Leach depicts so tellingly. I am spending three weeks at the National Humanities Center in Research Triangle Park, North Carolina. It is a wonderful place to work but, of course, I also needed a place to sleep. The good staff at the Center found what I was looking for — convenient, fully furnished, safe. It is also limboish, a vast place where there are no distinctive markers differentiating blocs or units. Because temporary, there is no particular incentive for dwellers to add individual or idiosyncratic markers to their upscale brand X units. Research Triangle Park is filled with such complexes, with names like "The Hamptons," conjuring up exotic playgrounds of the rich and famous. I turned into one such complex my first day here and meandered for five minutes before I realized it was not the

Leach contrasts radical mobility — whether of the affluent or the marginal and even desperate — with what it means to be committed to a place, to one's concrete neighbors, to an actual, not a virtual, community. But what we have done and are doing as a culture undermines commitments of stewardship in favor of looking out for number one — one's self, one's company. If there is a better deal elsewhere, one's loyalty, an evanescent thing in any case, is available to the top bidder as one quickly "relocates" in every sense of the word. Individuals are on the move; capital is on the move. Individuals may be growing richer, or at least many are, and capital is certainly growing stronger — with the greatest merger movement in American history starting in the 1980s and continuing to the present.[3] We accept no intrinsic barriers to this self-striving, meaning that we find it very difficult to think of any rationale that might involve taming acts of self-overcoming. The dominant forces of contemporary culture encourage the opposite habits and frames of mind in constituting a notion of our untrammeled self-sovereignty. But does this process make us weaker — or stronger? Americans don't feel powerful. They see themselves as caught in the maw of work, consumption, more work, more consumption — oh, we need a bigger house — on and on. "Isn't this what one does in America?" they tell themselves.

I have addressed this theme before, in a book called *Augus-*

---

one I "lived" in. And, of course, I got lost inside my own complex more than once before I found a way to orient myself and locate my "own" unit. The interior is nicely furnished and entirely faux, replete with a fake tree in a corner of the living room, fake French impressionist paintings on the walls. Driving in and out I have seen few children and no elderly. This looks like a place for yuppies, whether single or paired. All the units have the same paint, the same cars in parking lots. As I said, limboish. "Beyond America" for Leach is not, of course, a narrow chauvinistic sentiment but, rather, a way to get at the too-frequent disavowal of our responsibility for the place that is our home.

3. On this see Leach, *Country of Exiles,* pp. 40ff.

tine and the Limits of Politics.[4] Permit me to rehearse just a bit of what I have argued previously as a way to frame the discussion to follow, keeping ready to hand the views of our fallen condition unpacked in the first chapter. Bear in mind that my argument is not against the appropriate use of our freedom or our canny intelligence. As God's creatures, part of our birthright is "an element of independence and self-development," in Dietrich Bonhoeffer's words, a domain of action appropriate to the "relative freedom of natural life." But, Bonhoeffer also adds, within this freedom "there are . . . differences between the true and the mistaken use of freedom, and there is therefore the difference between the natural and the unnatural."[5] The natural is that form of life "directed towards justification, redemption and renewal through Christ."[6] Precisely because enactments driven by what Christians call pride, or a perversion and distortion of life, are always presented in the guise of freedom, it is vital to catalog the many ways in which pride distorts our appreciation of freedom.

Let us turn briefly to Augustine, who alerts us to false pride of the sort that "lurks even in good deeds to their undoing."[7] False pride turns on the presumption that we are the sole and only ground of our own being. We deny our birth from the body of a woman. We deny our dependence on her and others to nurture and tend to us. (Self-made persons cannot recognize and honor *constitutive* dependencies and interdependencies by contrast to those that are quite provisional and should eventually be relinquished.) We deny our continuing dependence on friends and family to sustain us. Pride denies our multiple and manifold

4. Notre Dame: University of Notre Dame Press, 1996.
5. Bonhoeffer, *Ethics,* p. 144.
6. Bonhoeffer, *Ethics,* p. 145.
7. The discussion of Augustine that follows is drawn from chapter 3, "Against the Pridefulness of Philosophy," in my *Augustine and the Limits of Politics.* All quotations from Augustine here are footnoted in that work.

dependencies and would have us believe that human beings can be masters of their fates. Those who refuse to recognize the many ways that they are dependent on others are themselves often overtaken by an urgent need to dominate, to "secure the dependence of others," according to Peter Brown, discussing Augustine.[8]

We seek to become our own point of origin. We fancy ourselves as the "Selfsame," to use Augustine's way of referring to an image of perfect completeness that perdures unchanged and is the same yesterday, today, and tomorrow. Consider our animus against aging and all the visible *signs* of aging. The currents of this fear of growing old propel us into a flight from time itself and prompt a desire to "fix" something, even if only "the self," securely in space. But Selfsameness, exert oneself as one might, is beyond the capacity of those like ourselves caught in mutability and temporality. Forgetting our natures as begotten and mortal, we easily become proud and self-absorbed. We may even be driven to become avid and destroyers, as Bonhoeffer claims. For if we are independent in all things, there is no need for us to humble ourselves. In a world framed by false pride, we are neither Bonhoeffer's torn creatures who must throw ourselves upon the cross, nor are we those whom John Paul II depicts as yearning wistfully for a more integral self. Instead, we normalize our audacity and call it good.

Acts of freedom, undertaken from faith and in love, are acts that recognize a limit. Acts of perverted freedom, undertaken from self-overcoming willfulness, recognize no limit. The latter leads to what Bonhoeffer called the "aberration and the mechanization of life. Here the individual is understood only in terms

---

8. Peter Brown, the distinguished historian of the late antique world, is author of *Augustine of Hippo* (Berkeley: University of California Press, 1969), a biography that remains the standard treatment of Augustine's life.

of his utilizable value for the whole, and the community is understood only in terms of its utilizable value for some higher institution or organization or idea. The collectivity is the god to whom individual and social life are sacrificed in the process of their total mechanization."[9] And life that posits itself as an absolute becomes its own destroyer. Such vitalism — again, according to Bonhoeffer, "cannot but end in nihilism . . . a misconceived absolutization of an insight which is in itself correct, namely, that life is not only a means to an end but is also an end in itself."[10]

HOW, as a culture, do we deny this and not only fall into but normalize the sin of pride? We do this, as I suggested above, in refusing to recognize any intrinsic limits to our own projects. I am going to take up one area in which this is so, that of economics.[11] Better put, perhaps I should say that an area in which the temptation to embrace false notions of freedom may, at times, be overweening is the world of money, property, possession, commerce — now extended to incorporate *all* areas of human existence. Human existence and spheres of social existence once deemed "off-limits" to the "money world" are no longer; markets, advertising, the cash nexus are pervasive. There are no longer barriers to the market's penetration into all areas of life, from cradle to grave.

Consider, first, our extraordinary national preoccupation with money. Money promises self-sufficiency: nothing can "touch us," as the saying goes, if we have enough. Or more than enough. For one can never have enough, as there are no mea-

9. Bonhoeffer, *Ethics,* p. 149.
10. Bonhoeffer, *Ethics,* p. 149.
11. This seems especially important at a moment in our national life when our collective well-being is measured by how the Dow Jones has done on any particular day.

sures for when an appropriate cut-off point has been reached. Why is that? Because, in part, one can never be too independent in all things, therefore not reliant intrinsically, by contrast to thinly and contingently, on the love and affection of others. Further, the more the better because this indicates one is among the winners rather than the losers in the game of life: one is not what is gently called "one of the also-rans of the human race." Money is also convenient. It helps us avoid sticky transactions and it protects slick ones. This is not, on my part, a moralistic brief against people's attempts to improve their lives. In the words of John Paul II: "It is not wrong to want to live better; what is wrong is a style of life which is presumed to be better when it is directed towards 'having' rather than 'being,' and which wants to have more, not in order to be more but in order to spend life in enjoyment as an end in itself."[12] John Paul suggests that the richer we get in this consumerist way, the poorer we become in a richly human way. That is why he insists that every decision to buy, spend, or invest is a moral and cultural choice, not just an individualistic preference. He shows us how a fleshed out theological and philosophical anthropology can help us to articulate the human freedom and dignity that is ours and that is not dependent on the latest, the fastest, the glitziest, the most expensive. Only in this way can we articulate and defend a concept of *enough*, a limit.

But our monied economy makes it far easier to desocialize economic life. Money can be transferred quickly and quietly and without the fuss of actually having to deal with a fellow human being in a palpable, tactile way. We can use money to make more money — fast — by manipulating symbols and sending those symbols round the world in milliseconds. To be sure, the world

---

12. Pope John Paul II, *Centesimus Annus, Encyclical Letter on the Hundredth Anniversary of Rerum Novarum* (Boston: St. Paul Books, 1991), p. 53.

was cumbersome indeed before money, especially paper money, got invented. Our forebears engaged in the tedious business of trekking cross-country, getting into unreliable boats, hauling goods or heavy ingots hither and yon, only, perhaps, to find themselves face-to-face with people they found both hostile and incomprehensible. That was very risky. What we moderns risk with money is, well, money. But, we are assured, fortunes are as quickly made as they are lost in the new global market. Without money we could not get what we want, as Marx, in one of his more lucid moments, pointed out. With apologies to the reader for the vulgarity of Marx's example, Marx argued that one attraction of the rather disembodied world of capital is that it enables an ugly man to buy a beautiful woman — that, in a sense, money is the great beautifier, the ultimate aphrodisiac. Consider that in our centers of power and finance, powerful men on the rise who want to be seen and photographed at events in a way that adds to their allure make use of the services of businesses that rent out beautiful, well-turned-out models to grace the arms of these men. Such women, whose names may be unknown to the men who rent them, are called "arm candy." Vulgar reality seems to have caught up with Marx's vulgar comment. Money appears to have both beautifying and cleansing properties — it puts a sheen on things. Money could get one from steerage to first class on the Titanic. We know how that story ended.

Is our own love affair with monied consumerism (by which I mean a distortion of legitimate activities and concerns) fueled by a proud quest for self-sufficiency, a variation on Augustine's famous *libido dominandi,* or lust to dominate, doomed to end as badly as the voyage of the great ship? Apocalyptic predictions are not my stock-in-trade, although warnings can and should be issued, remembering Bonhoeffer's haunting words: What is to come? It is yet possible — it is *always* in principle possible — for us to remember that we are creatures and finite but, for all that,

46

that our dignity is God-given and not for sale. That means we must steadfastly and resolutely combat the insistence that everything has a price and is commodifiable. But how do we do that given that such a refusal is a harder and harder sell (if you will forgive me) in a culture in which images of luxuriant, unencumbered self-sufficiency are part of the very air we breathe?[13]

LET'S PROBE a pervasive late modern habit of thought that now takes shape as something akin to an all-embracing ideology. I refer to the nexus: consumerist-commodifiable. Nothing is holy, sacred, or off-limits in a world in which everything is for sale.[14] It used to be that some things, whole areas of life, were not up for grabs as part of the world of buying and selling. Adam Smith and the great classical economists never advocated marketizing all aspects of human life, even as they insisted that the market itself required moral limits and frameworks. No more. Nowadays we find respectable and no doubt decent people in business, law, and the academy arguing for a free market in nearly everything, even babies. Not a "black market," mind you: that signifies shame, and we have nothing to be ashamed of. We would rid ourselves of shame as if it were a dotty old relative who gets in the way and makes a nuisance of himself or herself. Sin we construe as outmoded, in any case. Now we have syndromes

13. See the wonderful discussion on finitude and anxiety in Robin Lovin, *Reinhold Niebuhr and Christian Realism* (Cambridge: Cambridge University Press, 1995).

14. Marilynne Robinson, in a lively essay on Darwinism, shows the ways in which Darwinian presuppositions fed one school of economics (as the "dismal" science), namely, the Malthusian school. A constitutive feature of this approach is the insistence that: "There is no such thing as intrinsic worth. No value inheres in whatever is destroyed, or destructible" (*The Death of Adam* [New York: Houghton Mifflin, 1998], p. 33).

rather than, following temptation, a fall into sin. So it is an open market we seek as yet another sign of our new-found liberation from ancient prejudices. Families, religious faith, the law, bodies and body parts: all are redescribed in econometric terms. John Paul calls this a "structure of sin." How does it work?

One entry point is afforded by a recent work by a respected law professor who sees herself as a critic of the commodification school associated with the "law and economics" movement. In *Contested Commodities: The Trouble with Trade in Sex, Children, Body Parts, and Other Things,* Margaret Jane Radin takes up the presuppositions that undergird this pervasive school of thought and subjects these presuppositions to scrutiny.[15] But something goes wrong on the way to critique. Let me explain. Radin begins energetically: it simply is not the case that everything has a price. She resists "excessive commodification" through a "pragmatic philosophical and legal approach." The beginning premises of such an approach are nominalistic and conventionalist: Radin uses the pervasive term *social construction*. We are in deep water already, from the perspectives of theological and moral realism embodied, respectively, in the positions articulated by Bonhoeffer and John Paul II. For the "social construction" position opens up all claims — whether about what can be done to persons or what cannot — to arbitrariness, as the only limit to what we can do to or for persons is a pragmatic cut-off point, itself a strictly conventional artifact. Because human beings, in this scheme of things, are seen primarily as creatures responding to desire, and these desires are, in principle, unrestricted, the only question becomes: how and why do we arbitrarily restrict — "arbitrarily" because no restriction has the full force of law in anything other than a utilitarian and conventionalist sense. This is a complicated way of saying that one winds up not with the ques-

15. Cambridge: Harvard University Press, 1996.

tion of a framework that enables us to evaluate human goods but with a lowered, immanentist horizon (in effect, no horizon at all), within which we contest endlessly about what it is we want and rightfully deserve.

So Radin begins, noting that if Karl Marx is on one end (as a universal noncommodifier), then Gary Gecker and Richard Posner are on the other (as universal commodifiers).[16] Radin wants to find a middle way, but she does not find it in "traditional liberalism" because liberal philosophy, reflecting certain holdovers from a Christian and natural law backdrop (though Radin does not point this out), claims that some spheres of life are noncommodifiable in principle rather than just contingently, or for the moment. For Radin — a *critic,* remember, of the reigning commodified-consumerist vision — this is problematic, as it invites a view that holds that some spheres of life are off-limits to commodification and this claim may be just a cover-up to sustain gender discrimination, or to perpetuate some other nefarious or dubious scheme. Thus, in principle, *nothing is off-limits.* But, pragmatically, some things should be because human beings have come to "value" certain things. *Nothing, in her world, is valued for its own sake.* Value is an exclusively anthropocentric enterprise in which at least some human beings, if not all, would hold some things outside the market because these things (like babies) should not be "treated" as commodities. They should not because we "value" babies a certain way. So Radin frets about selling "infants and sperm, eggs, embryos, blood, organs, sexuality, pain, labor." Should all or none "come under a market regime"? It cannot be all or none, she insists. There must be some restraint, but under the right circumstances pretty much all re-

16. I should note that Marx's status as a noncommodifier is not grounded in a strong normative view of persons and their good. Marx is quite vague in such matters.

straints melt away for Radin, as we shall see. If *all* one can muster are so many pragmatic cut-off points for why draw a line here — or there — one has lost the wherewithal nessary to articulate and to defend a rich view of the dignity of persons and of why their bodies should not be subjected to certain uses and abuses. Absent a strong anthropology, there is no sturdy rationale for drawing and defending limits.

Thus, Radin argues, those who advocate an absolute ban on what are called "desperate exchanges," like selling a kidney because one is poor, may indeed be demonstrating no real respect for persons in such desperate circumstances. Why? Because persons who argue against organ sales may add "insult to injury" if they prohibit such sales entirely. They could be guilty of (hypothetically) starving a mother and her children, folks who might not have starved if a Bangladeshi mother had been able to sell her kidney to a Paris buyer. But think of the implications of this way of arguing. If we say: selling organs is a terrible but permissible instance of commodification under situations of desperation, and we should, therefore, legalize such transactions, we disarm ourselves. We make it harder to take a strong stand against the selling of kidneys. The best way to make the moral point is to say that it is dreadful for kidneys in Bangladesh to go to wealthy payees in the West. Thus we must never legalize this sort of thing. This does not mean we punish the desperate seller; it does mean we would, if we could, punish mercenaries who trade in organs for profit. If we say we cannot do any such thing because we are adding "insult to injury" for desperate people and because we are, in general, worried about a "maldistribution of wealth," we tacitly promote the view that, worried about maldistribution as we are, we proclaim in effect: Let them sell kidneys! Another line drawn in the sand is effaced as the rushing waters of commodification rise.

Surely the line must be drawn at baby selling! No, not even

here, it seems. Or, at least, the line may be drawn here but it is a pragmatic cut-off point only, hence provisional. Here is how that argument works. Suppose a poor woman wishes to sell a "baby on the black market" even as she may "wish to sell sexual services, perhaps to provide adequately for other children or family members." (Radin always imagines a benign purpose for this sale of self or others — never something like supporting a drug habit and the like.) Selling sexual services? Yes, this can be justified on some level. But there is a problem with selling babies, she admits. Why? Because of the intrinsic dignity and worth of babies? No, rather, because babies *cannot choose*. As a result, baby selling seems like slavery to us. But if choice is the heart of the matter — as it is in the commodified-consumerist ideology — then how do we justify the old practice of adoption? Here babies are given — released for adoption — even though, being babies, they have not chosen. So, Radin continues, if we forbid baby selling maybe we must forbid adoption too. If parents are "morally entitled to give up a child," and if we are opposed to trading in human flesh, why should not we forbid all exchanges, whether commodified or not? The only way out of this dilemma for Radin is that adoption remains lodged in a "nonmarket vision of human beings," and we have placed value on sustaining some aspects of this vision. Adoption fits this vision in a way that baby selling does not. But this is very thin as a grudging acceptance of adoption, to say the least. Radin has lost all access to a great, animating perspective that stresses the gift of love, hospitality, and succor to strangers in our midst; a love that welcomes without buying or selling a vulnerable child into a home.

Much of this discussion may sound extreme or outrageous to the reader unfamiliar with just how pervasive is this mode of thinking — a mode Radin, remember, aims to distance herself from. But the reader should not draw comfort in supposing this is such extreme stuff that it surely implicates just a few folks in the academy. In fact, we are all of us caught up in multiple ways in the world Radin displays (at times inadvertently) and analyzes; and, if I am right in this, it means we are all implicated in the triumph of a culturally sanctioned form of pride to which we are called, as children, to become habituated and, as adults, go on to practice. We do this given the habits we have formed. In the words of John Paul II: "A given culture reveals its overall understanding of life through the choices it makes in production and consumption. It is here that *the phenomenon of consumerism* arises. In singling out new needs and new means to meet them, one must be guided by a comprehensive picture of the person which respects all the dimensions of his being and which subordinates his material and instinctive dimensions to his interior and spiritual ones. If, on the contrary, a direct appeal is made to human instincts [as in advertising pitched at children] — while ignoring in various ways the reality of the person as intelligent and free — then *consumer attitudes and lifestyles* can be created which are objectively improper and often damaging to the person's physical and spiritual health."[17]

In other words, the form this pride takes is a sin of the masses, not a phantasm reserved to the elite. The world here depicted is seductive, and it is not all "bad," not by any means. I am arguing against dominant trends and the particular cultural forms that our economy in late modernity has taken. There is and has been historically extraordinary energy and vibrancy in the world of capitalism and markets. God certainly wants us to work and to better our lives. But we have arrived at a terminus within which the dominant questions are all of a pragmatic nature — or that is the way they are put. We assume the market in principle covers all and then we say: is there anything we should exempt? We are starting at the wrong end, so to speak, with pos-

17. John Paul II, *Centesimus Annus,* p. 52.

sible outcomes that have considerable "utility" rather than with a strong view of the human person from which intrinsic, not provisional, limits to certain sorts of human activities may then flow. John Paul notes the form of forgetting here inscribed: "Humankind, which discovers its capacity to transform and in a certain sense create the world through its own work, forgets that this is always based on God's prior and original gift of things that are. People think that they can make arbitrary use of the earth, subjecting it without restraint to their wills, as though the earth *did not have its own requisites and a prior God-given purpose, which human beings can indeed develop but must not betray* [emphasis mine]. Instead of carrying out one's role as a cooperator with God in the work of creation, a person sets himself up in place of God and thus ends up provoking a rebellion on the part of nature, which is more tyrannized than governed by him."[18]

There is so much we have shoved into the dank nooks and crannies of our culture, relegated to those musty corners where things we think we can do without are stored. Thus core distinctions marked by Augustine — *frui* and *uti* — are occluded. *Frui* means to enjoy and to cling with love to something for its own sake; *uti,* by contrast, is a form of use, employing something in order to obtain that which we love, provided it is worthy of love. Christians are not forbidden from using or making use of something for the sake of something else that is worthy of love. Rather, a Christian approach to an economy affords criteria that enable human beings to evaluate *good* from *ill* use, including the good or ill use of persons. When everything has a price and nothing any longer has dignity, the distinctions Augustine offered have collapsed. We have simply abrogated what D. Stephen Long calls the "first task of any Christian reflection on the economy," namely, "not to speculate whether Christian-

18. John Paul II, *Centesimus Annus,* p. 54.

ity sides with capitalism or socialism but to seek to interpret our 'economic activity,' that is, our producing, buying, selling, and consuming, within the larger narrative of God's economy. The first question Christian theologians should ask is, Given God's economy toward us, how does our inevitable participation in the material goods of this world reflect that economy? God's economy does not imply a blueprint for how Christians should organize the world economically. It does not give us any specific public policy easily translatable into terms either Capitol Hill or Wall Street will find useful. This is not surprising because God's economy is ultimately *not about the profitability of things but about their proper enjoyment.*"[19] Marilynne Robinson adds that: "The Judeo-Christian ethic of charity derives from the assertion that human beings are made in the image of God, that is, that reverence is owed to human beings *simply as such,* [emphasis mine] and also that their misery or neglect or destruction is not, for God, a matter of indifference, or of merely compassionate interest, but something in the nature of a sacrilege."[20]

But "proper enjoyment" is abandoned as a guide when we marketize everything, when we no longer have a way to distinguish good from ill use, when we can no longer discern what it means for something to be loved and enjoyed for its own sake. In his recent book, *Everything for Sale: The Virtues and Limits of Markets,* social and economic analyst Robert Kuttner analyzes a paper that aims to "dispatch the issue of slavery by branding it economically inefficient" — the closest one can get to Augustine's ill use in the commodified worldview — and that is the gravest indictment the paper's authors bring against the institu-

19. D. Stephen Long, "Charity and Justice: Christian Economy and the Just Ordering of the Commandments," *Communio* 25 (spring 1998): 14-38; quotation, p. 26.

20. Robinson, *Death of Adam,* pp. 47-48.

tion.[21] Kuttner discusses this paper in order to display what can happen when narrow economism as a habitual way of thinking takes over. The argument works like this, according to Kuttner: slavery was inefficient not only for the slaves but also for observers of slavery who suffered from "uncompensated third party effects" — that means they felt bad knowing that other human beings were enslaved; their capacity for empathy was still intact. So this bad feeling is reckoned as a cost — an "externality" — and slavery is criticized with a poof ball rather than being indicted with a moral mallet. A resounding critique of slavery clearly requires going outside econometrism-as-ideology. But this those in thrall to the economistic worldview are loathe to do. As Wittgenstein might say, "A picture holds them captive." This picture includes, though this is not spelled out, a very low anthropology, one in which persons are *not* intrinsically precious and dignified; rather, it shows a world in which individuals place value based on how best to maximize their utilities and given their preferences.[22]

Thus, for example, if one wants to talk about public goods and political life in a world in which everything is up for sale, one embraces something called "public choice theory." That means one behaves the way one behaves in the market because *everyone* in this world is driven by the same urgent need for self-sufficiency; everyone always maximizes his or her own self-interest, narrowly construed. If a person claims that other goods

21. All quotes are drawn from Kuttner, *Everything for Sale: The Virtues and Limits of Markets* (New York: Knopf, 1997).

22. Deirdre N. McCloskey, herself a participant in the world of academic economics, issues some warnings about certain pervasive habits and institutionally rewarded obsessions (on her view) of economics as a profession. This is a highly readable book and helpful, as she knows economics inside out. See Deirdre N. McCloskey, *The Vices of Economists: The Virtues of the Bourgeoisie* (Amsterdam: Amsterdam University Press, 1996).

are at stake, and that he or she is not animated across the board by this version of self-interest, that person is deluding him- or herself.[23] Public choice theory deals with the implications of this for politics. Many useful insights can, and have, been derived from public choice theory. The problem, again, is when a theory is stretched to cover *every* aspect of our private and public lives and becomes, thereby, an all-encompassing ideology, one compelled to deny all capacious views of politics by insisting that these can, in principle, be reduced to the terms of the theory. The demand that all forms of theory, research, and reasoning, in order to have validity and credibility, *must* conform to a certain philosophy, epistemology, and methodology, is itself the sin of philosophical pride.

Let me provide an example of how this works drawn from my experience in the academy. Some years ago at a university where I was then teaching, an eager young job candidate came through. He was a political scientist deeply immersed in the public choice model. Everything was a "preference" and could be described in the language of maximizing utilities. There was simply no other way to talk about politics. Everything was about winning at someone else's expense. There was simply no other way to talk about politics. Mantra-like, this went on for an hour. When he had finished, I asked: "Curious thing. When Martin Luther King delivered his great speech, he cried: 'I have a dream,' not 'I have a preference.' How do you explain this? Is there a difference?" Silence, then a bit of throat clearing. Finally, he responded that the Southern Christian Leadership Conference — I provided the name — was just like any other "interest group," so there really was no difference in principle. There are

---

23. This puts me in mind of a *New Yorker* cartoon featuring two dogs drinking at a bar. The one, leg crossed, drink in hand, says to the other: "You know, it's not enough that dogs win. Cats must lose."

many intelligent public choice theorists who understand that the question I put is not resolved quite so simply. But too few are ready to challenge a view that is, at one and the same time, closed yet aspires to be all-encompassing. So public life turns into a project of "adjusting preferences" at the margins and the language of "justice, virtue, charity, ethics, public-mindedness" — Kuttner's litany — falls by the wayside in favor of relentless commodification. Indeed, we have reached the point where the sweep and scope of commodification — what's for sale? — divides what might be called social Burkeans from economistic libertarians, although all get called "conservative."

WHERE DOES the Christian tradition place us in relation to all of this? Because Christians are called to relationality and to recognition of interdependencies, it follows that self-interest must be tempered by other, more social concerns. But this recognition is under tremendous pressure to succumb within a surround that places all of us inside a whirligig of relentlessly generated "wants" that translate rapidly into "needs." We are soon caught in a vicious circle. We pursue more material satisfaction because we need (read: want) more. But the more we want, the more we "maximize preferences"; and the harder we have to work or pay others to do work for us, the less time we have for children, for spouses, for friends, for church, for civic life, for solitude and reflection.

Consider how far along a certain cultural road we have traveled thus far. At present, we trust neither government nor one another.[24] Surely one reason trust is so low among us is that

24. On this and other aspects of our civic state see the reports of the Council on Civil Society and the National Commission on Civic Renewal. They are entitled, respectively, "A Call to Civil Society" and "A Nation of Spectators."

commitments are so casually breached. Writes Kuttner: "The person who volunteers time, who helps a stranger, who agrees to work for a modest wage out of commitment to the public good, who desists from littering even when no one is looking, who forgoes an opportunity to free ride, begins to feel like a sucker."[25] Our sociability suffers as a result, as does our capacity for solitude (by contrast to isolation). We cannot stand being alone but we have no time for others. Strange indeed. As a result, it seems entirely too possible that the glimpse John Paul affords us of the integral nature that eludes us may be eclipsed and that Luther's (and Bonhoeffer's) mordant view that reason retains *no* essential integrity after the fall comes into view as only too true. But if the latter is true, where do we derive any sturdy understanding to contrast what is natural, meet, and right with what is indecent, distorted, and sinful?[26]

Here is one final example of why economics seems to warrant the label "the dismal science," namely, a method devised for "costing out" the value of a human being's life, a distorted activity by any decent measure. We require two scales, one called

25. Kuttner, *Everything for Sale,* pp. 62-63. We have certainly not plummeted to the depths entirely. Even game-theory experiments launched in the expectation that each individual would free ride and "hope that somebody else will worry about the general welfare" show that large numbers of folks retain a residual bad conscience about a world that legitimates winning without limit and would, for example, "contribute a share of windfall winnings to the public good," this quite in opposition to the predictions and expectations of the dominant theory. Kuttner insists, and I believe he is right, that the market is dependent in ways its celebrants cannot acknowledge on what he calls "extra-market values" like trust and decent self-limits. But these are fragile things, these "extra-market" norms, and they cede territory every day.

26. I have not yet worked out whether Bonhoeffer's view of reason and its fundamental corruption softens at all and whether his unfinished *Ethics* bespeaks a rather higher view of human possibility than does *Creation and Fall*. I will pursue this topic another time.

DFE (Discounted Future Earnings) and the other WTP (Willingness to Pay). The former scale "values a person's life by projecting the value of lifetime earnings lost because of premature death or disabling injury, and then discounts into present dollars to adjust for future inflation." The second metaphor literalizes those surveys in which people conjure abstractly with what they think life and health are worth. Put these together and we have a value we can assign to a life.

Problematic? More than that, surely, for those of us working from within the resources afforded by our alternative tradition. For one recognizes the pernicious potential implications of such a scale. It might be, for example, that a person with handicaps whose DFE is next to nil is costing society, and his or her death would yield a "net benefit."[27] Many, perhaps most, though I am not at all sure about that considering the popular support for Dr. Kevorkian, would resist this conclusion.[28] But on what grounds? For grounds we have to go outside market values narrowly construed. One might turn, then, to Scripture and to the great interpreters of Scripture and to a community that keeps alive a biblical tradition. But, if one is a utility maximizer of the totalistic sort, one is not going to do this. And we are all called to be utility maximizers nowadays and, at the same time, to forget or to deny or to distort the Christian tradition in order to make that tradition comport with the preference-aggregations approach or, sim-

27. Indeed, this was one of the several arguments made in the Germany of National Socialism to justify the so-called euthanasia program, the killing of persons with disabilities or ailments, whether mental or physical. On this horrid story see Michael Burleigh, *Death and Deliverance: 'Euthanasia' in Germany 1900-1945* (Cambridge: Cambridge University Press, 1994), the first full-length treatment in English of this sorry business.

28. And in light of the fact that his mendacious lawyer, Geoffrey Fieger, did garner the Democratic nomination for governor of Michigan, although he lost resoundingly. A tribute to the good sense of the voters, yes, but a disquieting straw in the wind nonetheless.

ply, to ignore the existence of any tension whatsoever. Faith commitments, the culture tells us, are "private," in any case, so we can keep these locked up in a bin. This is helpful if we hope to eliminate conflicts or minimize the occasions within which these might arise.

Think of the violence this does to our understanding, beginning with anthropological presuppositions, whether Bonhoefferian and "more" Lutheran or John Paulian and "more" Catholic. For these traditions of faith are in agreement that human life is God-given and not up for pricing and marketizing; that we are called to relationality and communion; that we are enjoined to be good stewards of a good creation; and that our awareness of our finitude, our creatureliness, and our fallibility forestalls any quest for self-sufficiency, including the holy grail of a "perfect market." For the market, like all human institutions, is distorted by sin. To pretend that it is not is to compound one sin with another: pride. What is at stake is our capacity to recognize and to enact appropriate projects consistent with our natures, fallen though they may be. Here the relational dimension of Christian understanding cannot be too heavily accented. Let us return, once again, to Augustine.

Augustine reasons thus: God did not begin with the human species as a collective but with singularity. With other creatures, whether those of solitary habit "who walk alone and love solitude," or those who are "gregarious, preferring to live in flocks and herds," he "commanded many to come into existence at once."[29] But not so the human person. Here God created "one individual; but that did not mean that he was to remain alone, bereft of human society. God's intention was that in this way the unity of human society and the bonds of human sympathy be

---

29. Once again, the interested reader should consult my *Augustine and the Limits of Politics,* pp. 101-3, for all precise quotations from Augustinian texts.

more emphatically brought home to man, if men were bound together not merely by likeness in nature but also by the feeling of kinship." What is important about the singular human starting point?[30] Augustine explains in book 14 of *The City of God*. He reiterates God's purpose — that "the human race should not merely be united in a society by natural likeness but should also be bound together by the 'bond of peace.'" Spread out on the face of the earth, living under many customs and distinguished by a "complex variety of languages, arms, and dress," all participate in that fellowship we call human society; all are marked by the point of origin from one. One of the first laws that emerged was the law of marriage, a tie that binds and that, in turn, makes possible wider affections: the filaments of affection must not stop at the portal to the *domus*.

Indeed, we learn about neighborliness and reciprocity from this first beginning, for this is how we all began following the creation of the first human being. "The aim was that one man should not combine many relationships in this one self, but that those connections should be separated and spread among individuals, and that in this way they should help to bind social life more effectively by involving in their plurality a plurality of persons. 'Father' and 'father-in-law,' for instance, are names denoting two different relationships. Thus affection stretches over a greater number when each person has one man for father and another for father-in-law." Augustine goes on to discourse about mothers-in-law and sisters-in-law and cousins and grandchildren and the spouses of all of these and pretty soon one has a substantial social network.

The social tie is "not confined to a small group" but extends "more widely to a large number with multiplying links of kin-

30. For the purpose of making this point, Augustine is privileging Genesis 2:24 rather than 1:27.

ship." With this extension in kinship come prohibitions. Marriage between cousins is one that Augustine cites. He explains: "Yet no one doubts that the modern prohibition of marriage between cousins is an advance in civilized standards. And this not only because of the point I have already made, namely, that the ties of kinship are thereby multiplied, in that one person cannot stand in a double relationship, when this can be divided between two persons, and so the scope of kinship may be enlarged. There is another reason. There is in human conscience a certain mysterious and inherent sense of decency, this is natural and also admirable, which ensures that if kinship gives a woman a claim to honour and respect, she is shielded from the lust . . . which, as we know, brings blushes even to the chastity of marriage." (By "lust" Augustine refers to sinful possession that can occur even within a marriage.)

The upshot would seem to be this: any society that loses something of this sense of naturalistically grounded decency, of delicate yet sturdy relationality, is a society in trouble. The importance of plurality, of the many emerging from a unique one, cannot be underestimated in Augustine's work. "From one" creates a fragile but real ontology of relative peacefulness. Bonds of affection tie human beings one to the other, bonds that were not severed altogether with the fall and that we yearn for in our post-lapsarian state. Here John Paul's image of the fall into history that carries with it an anthropological yearning for greater wholeness and relationality is apt — and very far removed from the autarkic and selfish presuppositions of a world in which all relations can be priced. These latter presuppositions violate a fundamental norm of a specifically Christian understanding of membership in the human community. Writes Peter Burnell: "The characteristics of citizenship either specified or implied by Augustine to be good are its provision of the maximum range of relationships, that it is both large and subordinative, its basis in agreement as to what is loved, the decisive importance of the intensity with which that love is exercised, the origin of its cohesion in the justice of that love, the ultimately religious nature of that justice, its connection with the Divine Incarnation, its vital interest in exercising correct human understanding, and the basis of its hierarchy in a selfless concern of citizens for each other."[31] We are so far removed from this Augustinian understanding that our eyes may well with tears as we gaze across the vast distance that separates a world in which everything is up for sale from the one Augustine here so lovingly limns.

For a world in which *everything* is up for sale — in actual fact, not just in theory — would be one in which we would violate the second of the two great commandments routinely: one cannot love one's neighbor if one is trying to "make a killing," as we gently put it, at his or her expense.[32] But I think that something even more disconcerting is going on. I submit that, in falling into pride and forgetfulness, we are in danger of losing what it truly means to love one another, not excluding our own children. I hear the murmurs of exasperation now: Surely not! We are appalled by any such suggestion. No decent human being, no decent family, no decent society forgets what it means to love a child. In fact, we Americans *adore* our children. We dote on them. We buy them things. We drive ourselves to the brink of exhaustion to provide for them. We cheer them on, urge them to achieve, push them into precocious situations, pat ourselves on the back that they seem "grown up" at increasingly tender ages.

31. Peter Burnell, "Augustine and the Eternal Civility of Human Beings," unpublished ms., 1998, p. 20.

32. I would submit that it requires that we violate the first of these commandments as well. For the market in a world in which everything is for sale is godlike, the source of value. We cannot love the Lord our God with all our strength and might and from the depth and fullness of our being if we are worshiping at another altar.

"Children are so much more sophisticated now than they used to be," we hear. How, then, can we possibly have forgotten what is involved in loving a child? Our children are *indulged* beyond measure.

Of course, if we are honest, we admit that tens of thousands of American children walk on mean streets, attend schools that often resemble detention centers, get pregnant at early ages and without benefit of wedlock, and kill one another and themselves in unprecedented numbers. The teen suicide rate has tripled since 1960. Our teen pregnancy rate, though declining in the past few years, remains the highest in the Western world, nearly double that of our nearest competitor. We know that there is overwhelming empirical support for the popularly held view that where families and neighborhoods are intact, drug abuse (including alcohol), violence, teenage childbearing, and suicide among the young diminish. Because our basic sociality is under siege, families and neighborhoods are less and less likely to be intact. Unsurprisingly, all forms of socially and self-destructive behavior among our young people are either at unacceptably high levels or are on the rise. So all is not well. We are living in a post–Columbine High School world, and any who were complacent before April 20, 1999, find it difficult to be so at present. We know there is trouble out there.

Most people will grant this point. Yes, there are terrible problems. But we comfort ourselves that they have to do with the "structural" features of our situation, including poverty and despair. When it is pointed out that the problems noted above occur in affluent neighborhoods, too, we fall silent. Surely these are exceptions. Besides, this has nothing to do with whether we love our children. It has to do with the fact that we cannot protect our children from an excessively violent, materialistic, and individualistic culture. Parental love is not at issue. If love could save our kids, all would be saved. Or nearly all. Right?

It is not clear to me that we should comfort ourselves in this way. Pride enjoins this deflection from self-examination. Recognition of our fallenness, however, does not give us this out. I propose that we take a good hard look at how we love our children. But before I turn to this theme, let me be clear that I recognize the terrible binds in which American parents too often find themselves, in part because the world of work — and the money culture — has usurped so many other areas of life. Many aspects of our lives are effectively beyond our control. Consider the fact that more than 7 million Americans hold two or more jobs, up some 65 percent from 1980. The average worker spends 163 hours a year more working than in 1980 — that is a whole month stolen from family, church, and community. Some 71 percent of school-age children have no parent at home full-time compared with 43 percent in 1970, yet only 13 percent of mothers with preschool-age children say they want to work full-time. Moreover, our tax code is biased against parents. Between 1969 and 1983, average tax liability for singles and childless couples showed no significant increase. But the tax rate rose 43 percent for married couples with two children. So we have a culture tilted against concrete, hands-on time spent with children.[33] Having said that, I want to look at the many ways we find to rationalize this situation and not to consider what we might do, even with all the pressures here noted.

SOME YEARS ago now the notion of "quality time" gained credence. Designed to arrest surges of guilt and misgiving because we were spending less and less time with our children and in-

33. These dire findings derive from Cornel West and Sylvia Ann Hewlett, *The War Against Parents* (New York: Houghton-Mifflin, 1998). See also Reed Abelson, "Part-Time Work for Some Adds Up to Full-Time Job," *The New York Times* (2 November 1998): A1, A16.

creasingly giving our children over to others to care for, many helpful analysts, agents of the zeitgeist in this matter, hit on a handy idea: quality time. Not that old-fashioned sort of time with its complex, natural rhythms that flowed and bumped along as hours unfolded in which the task at hand might be work or play, baking cookies or learning how to ride a bike, taking a bath or taking a "time out," watching Mom or Dad in the kitchen, Mom or Dad gardening, reading books, doing home-work, doing nothing but doing it in one another's company. No, quality time was that little window of opportunity that emerged between, say, 7:00 and 8:30 p.m., after a rushed dinner and be-fore being sent to bed.

Why the rush? The answer is obvious. Because every adult in the home and the neighborhood was now in the paid labor force, children either shifted for themselves — and the hours of danger for all the troubles I noted above are unsupervised after-school hours — or awaited a harried parent at day care, or "after care." Mom or Dad raced home, raced through supper, and were then enjoined to engage in that magical moment — quality time. Somehow the snatches of quality time here and there made up for all the time apart, all the absences, all the harried, angry bits and pieces that made up the ever more typical day of ever more typical American parents. As economist Allan Carlson has pointed out, modern capitalism and modern states have a "vested interest" in family disaggregation: "Family bonds interfere with the efficient allocation of human labor, and household production limits the sway of a money-based economy."[34] In fact, much of "what we measure as economic growth since 1960 has simply been the trans-fer of remaining household tasks uncounted in monetary terms — home cooking, child care, elder care — to external entities such as

34. Allan Carlson, "Toward a Family-Centered Economy," *New Oxford Review* (December 1997): 28-35; quotation, p. 29.

Burger King, corporate day-care centers, and state-funded nursing homes."[35] This is called progress. Quality time is part and parcel of this monetizing of everyday life. Time is parceled out into measurable, hence more "efficient," chunks. And, as I have already indicated, we comfort ourselves that our children are really the winners. They are not. Children have been the big losers along with average American families.

What corporations have done by tapping into the "vast pool of married women for labor" is to drive down "the average industrial wage." So work becomes more and more a necessity. But this work barely keeps people's heads above water. Women predominate in low-pay, service-sector jobs. One low-pay job is child care. To be sure, there are many wonderful day-care centers staffed by loving people. Such centers are predominantly church-based. I have no interest in criticizing either day-care workers or overworked parents. But I do want to raise questions about our priorities and the many ways we, being human-all-too-human, fool ourselves into thinking all is well or even better when clearly all is not. Surely, however, decent and equitable relations between men and women need not entail a form of culturally sanctioned neglect or abandonment, literal or emotional, of children!

I have no doubt shocked if not angered many readers. So let me spell out what I have in mind. Love is tough-minded, hard work. Loving children, as caring mothers and fathers throughout the years have recognized, is about profound attention.[36] Attention requires *being there*.[37] One must be cued in to the nuances of

35. Carlson, "Toward a Family-Centered Economy," p. 29.

36. There are a number of what might be called philosophers of attention. Simone Weil comes to mind, and I would also suggest looking at the writings of the feminist philosopher Sara Ruddick.

37. I do not, of course, mean a kind of rigid scrutiny of the child at every moment. Rather I refer to an attentive way of being open to the concrete reality of the child and his or her uniqueness.

the child's needs as these change, sometimes from day-to-day in the case of babies and toddlers. When our granddaughter, a precocious five-year-old as of this writing, was fourteen months old, I journeyed to Colorado, where her family then resided, to care for her for a week as her mom took a course in fiber sculpting. (Our daughter, Heidi, is an artist.) I arrived eager to spend time with this lovely, intelligent little girl.[38] When I presented myself for care duty, my daughter handed me several sheets entitled: JOANN AT 14 MONTHS — GUIDELINES FOR CARE-TAKERS. Just reading these guidelines exhausted me, and I was reminded: this is what it means to love a child. This is the difference between loving attention and that indulgent, permissive attitude we often mistake for such. The point is not to "cater" to the child but to tend to the irreducible specificity of this one being, this child of God. We all need such attention paid, and, if we have received it, we are enjoined to return it in full measure, not as tit-for-tat but, as Luther argues, from the abundance of overflowing faith.

Here is a radically excised version of Heidi's guidelines, but these will suffice to demonstrate why quality time is such a distorting nostrum. Children need real time. That our society at *this* time draws nearly every adult out of home and community and into what is, for the vast majority, an often stressful world of work absent much in the way of ensured benefits, is an indictment of our society — not of the men and women trying to do their best to remain sane and decent within it.[39] What I am arguing is that a world in which everything is marketized makes it more difficult for people to remember what the work

38. What else? She is my granddaughter, and our grandchildren are precious to us in the most powerful ways. But there are "objective" criteria, for example, her ability to read at age 5.

39. I am not, by the way, assuming that everyone wants to be either sane or decent.

of love is all about. Here, then, are Heidi's guidelines (edited and shortened):

Diapers. Change almost every hour to hour and a half. Diaper covers in top basket behind counter door at changing station. Just dump soiled diapers in diaper bucket after rinsing in toilet. Let JoAnn flush the toilet.

Food. Any food that is cut up small enough that she will eat. NOTHING WITH NUTS. No peanut butter, etc. CUPS of milk and water and juice — use bottle at nap and sleep time and in car.

Nap. Is erratic. Try to follow routine that she is used to and it is OKAY for her to cry a bit.

Crying. JoAnn has very loud "cry outs" that last about a minute in between light sleep and heavy sleep. DO NOT RUSH TO CHECK ON HER WHEN SHE DOES THIS. Wait a minute, see if it is just that one yell. If she cries and continues for 5 minutes during her nap, then see nap time (below) on what to do next.

General Schedule. JoAnn wakes around 7 a.m. Change diaper, hold her, read books. (She wakes up slowly.) Then she likes to play for a little while. She will eat breakfast around 8-8:30 a.m. She does not eat much for breakfast. Examples of breakfast food: bananas, half a bagel with cream cheese, cheerios and milk, grits, cream of wheat, fruit, scrambled egg, piece of thin toast spread with cream cheese. ALWAYS give her prune juice in the transparent red cup. (That way you can see how much she has left to drink; she should drink all of this. If she does not drink it in one sitting, have her finish it at another time.)

Milk. Give her a CUP of milk during the day. Refill this cup as the day goes on.

START YOUR DAY. Go on a trip, go on an errand, visit one of the places below, outside is always a delight, reading, play.

Lunch. Around 11 a.m. Fix a plate with a veggie, fruit, string cheese, cottage cheese, mashed potato, turkey dog from freezer (defrost in microwave for 2 minutes and cut into tiny bits, always cut lengthwise in quarters), potatoes if some in fridge from cooking, yogurt, bread, crackers. She will do a pretty good job of feeding herself, but might need help scooping up the food with her spoon. Bibs and rags are far left drawer in kitchen, second one down.

Nap time. Is very erratic. If you were in town during morning or visiting someone and you traveled home around 11 a.m., then she probably fell asleep for a little while in the car. Then she most likely will not have another nap. Sometimes at noon I put on the lullaby tape as she drinks her bottle. Sometimes she still wants me to read until 12:30, and then she goes into her crib while she is wide awake, or she may fall asleep. If she cries check on her in 5 minutes. Do not pick her up. Tell her, "It's nap time and you need to go to sleep. I will be in the next room. You can go to sleep by yourself" and leave — quickly. She will probably still cry. Do not check on her (unless worried for her safety) for another 20 minutes; then do the same routine. She will usually just talk and play with her 4 toys in her crib and have "quiet time" for awhile. She will nap anywhere from 20 minutes to 2 hours. A key to whether she is really sleepy is if she starts getting VERY careless, reckless, and clumsy. Then try to get her down for a nap or quiet time.

Your day is still going. Try to sneak in 20 minutes of reading sometime.

Then followed more details, interspersed with the staccato repetition, a kind of caregiver's mantra: "Your day is still going." Bath and bedtime details included the following: "7:45 p.m. bath time for 20-30 minutes. Put her in plastic diaper, t-shirt, and pajamas. She gets uncovered almost every night so do put on a t-shirt under pajamas. Quiet time, lullaby tape, singing songs, a warm bottle. Never give her more than 2 bottles at this time of evening. Do not let her get down from your lap and start to play. Hold her until 8:30. Put her in crib whether asleep or not. She will cry for a few minutes, then go to sleep. If she has not had any nap or only a 20-minute nap she often falls asleep by 8 p.m. Move the above routine back by half an hour."

Then followed a list of THINGS TO DO WITH JOANN — early childhood center, playgrounds, an animal farm, and the like. We say the devil is in the details. So is love. Love is not a sentiment: it is a craft. I submit that we are forgetting this craft of love. We are too consumed with ourselves. Economic life in a distorted sense is driving us. In our frenzied lives, we cannot spend the time and attention required. Love is the heart of formation, of what it means to induct children into a way of life, to help them to understand what a decent, loving life is all about. But we know — on this score there can simply be no doubt — that our children are less and less formed in this attentive, painstaking, loving way and more and more given over to "structures" and cultural forces.[40] We want to believe we are doing the right thing. We give our children so many choices nowadays, we exclaim. But a two-year-old does not need five dozen options. He or she needs trust and love and the confidence that we are competent to do God's work on earth by holding and nurturing those born of our own acts of co-creation. This is the product of that attunement to the nitty-gritty details, to time in all its complexity, for it takes time to learn what children need, time to tend to the

---

40. Let me be clear: this is *not* a brief against any form of play care or day care. But it is an attempt to set as a norm for all forms of care the loving, concrete attention paid by loving parents to *this* child. As our notion of what care involves deteriorates, we seem more prepared than ever before just to hand children over, keep our fingers crossed, and soothe our consciences with "quality time" talk and the like.

tasks. We all need this sort of loving attention paid. The dignity of the human person lies in the fact that we are beings to whom a certain loving attention is owed. During that week in Colorado, JoAnn Paulette Welch's grandmother was reminded of this truth and brought up yet again to a recognition of the reality of the present moment, one in which we have so little time for those we love, beginning with our children.

HOW CAN this possibly be? How could we let this happen? For God — our God — so loved the world he gave his only begotten Son, so that we might have life and have it more abundantly; so that, from our fallenness, love might afford us a glimpse of the lushness and fullness of a community of reconciliation. We forgot — and it was no innocent forgetting. Prideful or totally preoccupied selves cannot make any space for others. A culture that generates forms of preoccupation of the sort that narrow the circles of human sociality is a culture that should be subjected to sustained critique if one is working with a different understanding of an economy. To treat this issue fully, it would be necessary to go on at this juncture to evaluate various Protestant and Catholic responses to economic life and pressures. This I cannot do in any great detail here. But a few comments are in order. Surely Bonhoeffer would ask us to think of orders of creation and whether some fundamental violation occurs when one area of life gobbles up so much that rightfully belongs to other aspects and dimensions of human existence. He would acknowledge the dire circumstances in which people find themselves and remind us of the demands of necessity.[41] At the same time, and in light of

41. But even here the Catholic tradition seems to have a more fully worked out set of notions about the precise content of necessitarian claims. For example, Vincent Carraud, in "Hatred of Theft, Love of Thief," *Communio* 25 (spring 1999): 4-13, unpacks the Thomistic distinction be-

the central importance of friendship and family to Bonhoeffer, any single-minded pursuit of economic gain, whether out of insecurity or avarice, would confirm for him just how fallen is our condition and reaffirm for him just how central to a decent ordering of human existence is "Christ the center" and a "life together" as part of a community of believers.

John Paul, heir to the complex tradition of Catholic social thought, has made clear his views on economic life in a number of important and powerful encyclicals: *Laborem Exercens, Centesimus Annus, Sollicitudo Rei Socialis.* Having written rather extensively on Catholic social thought, I refer the reader to other essays.[42] But this much needs to be said: the solidarity of persons and the theme of subsidiarity are the cornerstones of an alternative to a disordered economic life, including a distortion of work life. Perhaps Catholic thinking in this area is more richly developed than Lutheran tradition because the lingering intimations of integral nature generate a robust sociopolitical analogue: the notion of the common good. As the Synod of Bishops' "Working Paper" on America proclaims: "The Christian reality is complex because the ethic of justice and the requirement of fraternal solidarity must both be met. The Christian faith calls for a Christian social ethic, which the church's social doctrine proposes in a sys-

---

tween *extreme* necessity, such as danger for life, health, bodily integrity, and legitimate emergency, and *common* necessity, or deficiency of goods and material advantages, arguing that only the first is an excusing case for theft, for example. So theft to feed oneself or one's family is not even theft, if it is a matter of urgent necessity. Here, clearly displayed, is a primacy of justice over property. This held, according to Carraud, for both patristic and medieval scholars. The Lutheran tradition, of which Bonhoeffer is a glorious example, does not have a developed tradition of thinking about justice claims.

42. The best place to begin is with the encyclicals themselves, of course. Commentary on Catholic social thought is enormous. One of my own essays is "Individual Rights and Social Obligation," which appeared in German and in *Common Knowledge* 7, no. 3 (winter 1998): 117-28.

tematic way as directives for Christ's disciples in their personal, family, cultural and social life. . . . The social doctrine formulates the basic principles for viewing real situations and the criteria of moral judgment for evaluating the social conflict between the human reality and the Christian ideal as well as the rules capable of guiding the concrete actions of individuals and communities for the promotion of the common good and the overcoming of moral disorder and social injustice."[43]

In Catholic social thought, the person comes first and is prior to the formation of the state or of an economic order. That person is, as we have already seen, born into community. John Paul has been persistent and eloquent on what he calls, in *Laborem Exercens,* the "subjective" meaning of work. Or, better put, the human person as the subject of work. From this beginning, he mounts a powerful argument against economism and materialism. This approach seeps down to all levels of Catholic teaching. Thus, in a 1998 statement called "Life on the Land: A Call to Reflection and Action," the bishops of Ohio, commenting on the continuing crisis of the family farm and the move toward conglomerate "agribusiness," not only insist that all human beings have a right to basic essentials — like food — but that a "just" agricultural system is one that relies on "stewardship of the land" and the "dignity and fair treatment of all who work in the system." The bishops reject the deterministic argument that "we are captives of the economic forces of the marketplace. Concentration is said to be inevitable, bringing larger economies of scale and higher productivity and profitability. However, our economy remains a human creation, which reflects our choices about what we value. We must not lose sight of the fact that the economy exists to serve the human person, not the other way around. All

43. "Special Synod for America: The Working Paper," *Origins* 24, no. 3 (11 September 1997): 201-24; quotation, p. 217.

economic choices and institutions must be judged by how they protect or undermine the life, dignity and fundamental rights of the human person."[44] With this emphasis on dignity and fundamental rights ringing in our ears, consider the following two vignettes, two short notes on America separated by some eighty years or more.

A headline on the front page of *The New York Times* for March 19, 1998, proclaims: "4,000 Hearts Full of Hope Line Up for 700 Jobs." We learn of Gayle Blanding, who put on her best dress and kept repeating over and over again: "I have great confidence. I have great skills." But, the article tells us, the "38-year-old unemployed woman still trembled as she rode the A train from Harlem to midtown Manhattan yesterday, despite the fact that her 19-year-old daughter kept whispering into her ear: 'You're going to get that job.' Lasidy Honoret had taken an unpaid day off from his $5-an-hour cook's job in order to apply for a position as a staff member at the Roosevelt Hotel in midtown Manhattan, reopening soon after renovations. An eighteen-year-old kid? No, Mr. Honoret is 33, from the Dominican Republic, and a lawyer in his old life. He's worked in factories and supermarkets since he hit New York. He had had a dream of going to Harvard and of sending money back to his 71-year-old mother. But now he's mashing potatoes at a Boston Market and wondering why he left home." The reader gets the picture: an explosion of applications, four thousand people show up for seven hundred jobs. The article tells us that the police had to erect barricades to keep the crowd orderly.

For most of us this is a story tinged with pathos. Something is wanting here. Not just the fact that thirty-three hundred hopefuls will not get jobs, but the fact that the process is scarcely an

44. The bishops' call appears in *Origins* 27, no. 44 (23 April 1998): 734-37.

exercise in the dignifying of the human person. We are told that the market just works this way. But for us noneconomic types something is amiss. We think that a trained lawyer should probably be plying his craft rather than doling out mashed potatoes at a chicken chain. Perhaps the resonance of economic desperation, and how much on the razor's edge are so many among us, helps to account for the enormous success of the 1999 revival of Arthur Miller's classic, *Death of a Salesman,* at Chicago's Goodman Theatre. Willy Loman is a man made desperate by economic circumstance. What he has to sell nobody any longer wants. The solemn promise he had from the company's founder, father of the company's current head, that so long as the company existed Willy had a job, is not recognized as binding by the man's son. Willy reduces himself to begging. He will work for anything. But his employer hardens his heart. Willy, at the end of his tether, takes his own life. His beleaguered wife, at moments throughout the play, reminds us that "Attention must be paid." Yes, to a complex and by no means heroic figure like Willy, to grandchildren, to all of us.

This leads to my second economic vignette. A few of us recall tales told by our immigrant grandparents. My grandfather, who was bitter about this to his dying day, described his first Christmas Eve in America. A hired farmhand, though a boy age 10 or 11, he was forced to shovel frozen cow manure out of a barn on a bitter Colorado night, the icy blast off the dry plains chilling his bones and his spirit. He never got over it. It was not the hard, even brutal work that got to him — that was to be his lot for years. He, by then, recognized that this new country, this America, did not have streets paved with gold. His bewildered, poor family had been greeted by no welcoming committee. Those in Nebraska, then Colorado, who worked the immigrants but also derided them (at least some did), mocking their awkward attempts to speak the English language, had taught him that. No, it was not these indignities that fueled his lingering ire. It was that he was forced to work on Christmas Eve. Was nothing holy?

In the economistic-commodifiable world the answer, clearly, is no. Further, an economy that turns, at times brutally so, on winners and losers is one that refuses to recognize and to accept humanity in all its variety, including the many gifts each of us has to offer, not excepting those who cannot engage in what we call "productive" work. When everything is for sale, fundamental acts of recognition, of the sort John Paul II locates as central in the formation of our understanding of persons (beginning with the "recognition" of Eve after Adam's deep sleep), are effectively occluded or far more difficult to sustain.

If pride squeezes out the space for others, hence for an appropriate self-regard consistent with our recognition of others and the loving attention that should be paid to them, slothfulness is equally troubling. Sloth and pride would seem to be opposites: pride conjures up the notion of an ambitious, striving, bustling self, recklessly knocking over any barriers to self-promotion. Sloth, on the other hand, suggests indolence and an incapacity to act. Yet, as I shall argue, these two come together. Slothfulness is yet another way the fallen self refuses to pay proper attention and, in so doing, abandons the Christian freedom that is truly ours. Slothfulness, Luther assures us, is "one of the fruits of original sin." For "we are born with it by nature and it clings to us."[45] So it is to sloth and its current incarnations that we next turn.

45. Martin Luther, "Psalm 101" (trans. A. von Rohr Sauer), in *Luther's Works,* vol. 13: *Selected Psalms II,* ed. Jaroslav Pelikan (St. Louis: Concordia, 1956), p. 174 on Ps. 101:2.

LETTER TO GENETICALLY
ENGINEERED SUPER-HUMANS

You are children of our fantasies of form,
our wish to carve a larger cave of light,
our dream to perfect the ladder of genes and climb

its rungs to the height of human possibility,
to a stellar efflorescence beyond all injury
and disease, with minds as bright as newborn suns

and bodies which leave our breathless mirrors stunned.
Forgive us if we failed to imagine your loneliness
in the midst of all that ordinary excellence,

if we failed to understand how much harder
it would be to build the bridge of love
between such splendid selves, to find the path

of humility among the labyrinth of your abilities,
to be refreshed without forgetfulness,
and weave community without the threads of need.

Forgive us if you must reinvent our flaws
because we failed to guess the simple fact
that the best lives must be less than perfect.

FRED DINGS,
from *Eulogy for a Private Man*
(reprinted with permission of the author)

Chapter Three

Forgetting That We Are Fallen:
The Slothful Self

We do not think of sloth much anymore. The term *slothful* is rarely deployed, perhaps because it has such an archaic sound. "Lazy," yes, but even that has fallen into desuetude. We are more likely to psychologize our characterizations and to label someone with insufficient get-up-and-go, or one plagued by a kind of torpor where his or her own life is concerned, as plagued by low self-esteem. "Lazy" implies a "value judgment," and we are enjoined not to make such judgments any longer.

How rapidly things change — and not necessarily for the better. In one of the most popular Dr. Seuss books for children, *Horton Hatches the Egg,* our hero, Horton the elephant, takes over the arduous task of hatching an egg from "Mayzie, a lazy bird," who would rather play than work.[1] Mayzie tells Horton she will be gone but a short time. Horton takes over

---

1. Dr. Seuss, *Horton Hatches the Egg* (New York: Random House, 1940). One of the many joys of grandparenting is that one gets to renew one's acquaintance with wonderful books.

egg-hatching duty, and lazy Mayzie never returns. Horton sticks to his task through thick and thin, faithful despite terrible storms, freezing ice, the taunts of friends, and danger from elephant stalkers who, rather than shooting him, decide to haul Horton — tree, egg, and all — off to New York, where they sell him to a circus. The circus sends the elephant-hatching-an-egg act all over the country. Horton, humiliated, never budges because: "I meant what I said/And I said what I meant . . . ;/An elephant's faithful/One hundred per cent!"

When the circus to which Horton has been sold plays near Palm Beach, "Who . . . should chance to fly by/But that good-for-nothing bird, runaway Mayzie!/Still on vacation and still just as lazy." Lazy Mayzie's timing is impeccable — she arrives at the moment when the egg, after 51 weeks of faithful Horton sitting, begins to hatch. Horton excitedly cries "My EGG! WHY IT'S HATCHING!" Lazy Mayzie, now that all the work has been done for her, lays claim to the egg and lies that Horton has stolen it from her. Horton, forlorn, backs off just as the egg hatches. Out flutters an elephant-bird that looks exactly like Horton save this elephant baby has wings. Horton and his elephant-bird baby head home in triumph. Lazy Mayzie sulks in a corner.

Published in 1940, *Horton Hatches the Egg* is clearly intended as a Dr. Seuss meditation on the virtue of faithfulness and as a critique of laziness. These are lessons people continue to teach their children, or hope their children pick up along the way, I suspect, even as the wider culture has strayed.

To be sure, we enjoin people to be enormously, distractedly busy. But our busyness, strangely enough, may constitute its own version of laziness, as acquiescence in cultural forms that promote slackness of purpose as every moment of every day is gobbled up in a frenzy of activity and one sells self, goods, anything for whatever the market will bear.

Luther, as noted above, describes sloth as one of the fruits of original sin. It is part of our fallen heritage and "it clings to us." But what exactly clings and why is sloth a problem? The dictionary defines sloth as disinclination to action, or indolence. A slothful person is one who is sluggish. How can this possibly characterize anyone or anything in a cultural moment I have already characterized as frenzied, one in which we seem closer with each passing day and moment to Hobbes's reductive characterization of human beings as so much matter in constant motion? Have I not already offered up a series of pointed criticisms against excessive activity of the sort signified by the triumph of contemporary *homo economicus*? Yes, but that is part of the story of sloth. I take sloth to mean not simply inactivity but acquiescence in the conventions of one's day; a refusal to take up the burden of self-criticism; a falling into the zeitgeist unthinkingly, and, in so doing, forgetting that we are made to "serve God wittily, in the tangle of our minds." The upshot is that we lose the critical recognition that those called by the name "Christian" are poised between two poles: *contra mundum* and *amor mundi*. That is part of what it means to be "salt and light" to the world. In Volume 4 of his multi-volume masterwork, *Church Dogmatics,* Karl Barth offers powerful thoughts, mincing no words, on "The Sloth of Man." Sloth is sin, quite simply, and Barth describes it as "sluggishness, indolence, slowness or inertia." It is "evil inaction" by contrast to the "heroic, Promethean form of sin." Pride and sloth may seem antitheses but there is a "profound correspondence" between the Promethean and the "unheroic and trivial form of sloth." One is "evil action"; the other "evil inaction."[2] The human as sinner is "not merely Prometheus or Lucifer" but also "a lazy-bones, a sluggard, a good-for-nothing, a slow-coach and a loafer."[3] Sloth is a type of escapism, an evasion of re-

2. Karl Barth, *Church Dogmatics,* Vol. IV, Doctrine of Reconciliation (Edinburgh: T. and T. Clark, 1958), p. 403.

3. *CD,* IV, p. 404.

sponsibility. It comes down to a form of "practical atheism," for Barth, a kind of slothful denial of God and Creation. And sloth may well "disguise itself as ceaseless activity," as I will, in fact, argue about our "American" version of sloth, so to speak.[4]

What is at stake in each case — whether pride or slothfulness — is a negation of appropriate humility; a denial of relationality and community; a quest for self-sufficiency that, in the case of sloth, involves too thoroughgoing an absorption in the views and evaluations of others.[5] This wants explaining, for there is a chasm that separates Christian understandings of servanthood from, say, the slave side of Hegel's master/slave dialectic. The one — servanthood — posits that we grow as selves as our capacities for servanthood widen and deepen. The other — slavishness — means to be the possession of some other and, as well, to be caught in a scenario in which one's options are either slavery or domination, executioner or victim (to borrow Camus's phrase). The terrible irony of the latter is that, in order to be enslaved, one does not require a taskmaster poised to administer blows should one fail to do the master's bidding. One is akin to Kafka's bird in search of a cage. Slothful ensnarlment is complex because it derives from a deformation of deep needs and desires that help to constitute our humanity, including loving regard for the self and respect for others. This loving regard and concern for the views of others easily goes awry. Indeed, if one follows Lu-

---

4. *CD,* IV, p. 439.

5. Some interesting observations have emerged concerning the wildly disproportionate number of women dispatched by Dr. Kevorkian. Many of these women, it seems, were suffering from depression as much as anything else. All of them were so transfixed by the view that women are to minister to others but not to be ministered to themselves that they saw it as an act of salutary love to kill themselves with Kevorkian's help — at least so some critics have reasoned. Surely sloth — acquiescing in the view that women must always be so attuned to the view of others that they do not assert themselves — is implicated in this terrible phenomenon.

ther, all our needs are bound to be distorted in light of the fact that we are in rebellion against God, the source of undistorted love. Human reason and willing are corrupted through and through by original sin. Within Catholic teaching, natural reason has more ready access to certain truths about self or other, but such access can never aspire to perfection and luminescence.

LET'S TURN, then, to an examination of slothfulness as it seeps into the pores, sinews, and tissues of the ways in which we think about and treat the body in late modernity. The overarching and framing thematic is a flight from finitude that may at first blush seem but one additional moment of prideful triumphalism but, on closer examination, can be construed as implicating us in distorted and distorting forms of self-excision. What I refer to shorthandedly with the term *self-excision* is a type of self-abnegation that occludes recognition of the complexities and joys of embodiment — the "givens," if you will, of finitude and created being itself. One spin-off is widespread acquiescence in, even hearty approval of, destruction of the bodies of others as part of our culture's panoply of invented rights and punishments. To be more specific, the culturally and legally sanctioned projects I have in mind implicate us in direct or indirect self-loss through those state-sponsored and sanctioned acts of radical excision we know as abortion and the death penalty. Perhaps better put, I wish to draw attention to a cultural matrix of which these state-sanctioned acts of radical excision are direct outgrowths. If pride fetters us through inordinate self-mastery, the tentacles of sloth strangle us through forms of inappropriate self-loss. Either way, we abandon recognition of the many ways in which we are claimed by that which is other than ourselves, that which redeems us through the works of love in and through freedom and faith.

A number of issues have been summarily adumbrated. Let's flesh matters out, beginning with reminders about the nature of Christian freedom and the fact that we are both creatures and creators. As creatures we are dependent. It follows that our creaturely freedom consists in our recognition that we are not abstractly free but free only in and through relationship. A limit lies at the very heart of our existence in freedom. One is bound, at this point, to recall Luther's most famous words — after "Here I stand" — from his great essay, "The Freedom of a Christian": "To make the way smoother for the unlearned — for only them do I serve — I shall set down the following two propositions concerning freedom and the bondage of the spirit: 1. A Christian is a perfectly free lord of all, subject to none. 2. A Christian is a perfectly dutiful servant of all, subject to all."[6] Christian freedom turns on recognition of the limits to freedom.

Bonhoeffer, one may recall, frets that the human being *sicut deus,* as Creator, transmogrifies into a destroyer as he and she misuse freedom. At the same time, our freedom is a constitutive part of our natures. So: how do we understand this freedom? Robin Lovin helps us to appreciate a specifically Christian freedom, one that is not opposed to the natural order but acts in faithfulness to it.[7] We begin by taking human beings as they are, not as those fanciful entities sometimes conjured up by philosophers in what they themselves call "science fiction" examples.[8]

6. From "The Freedom of a Christian," in Timothy F. Lull, ed., *Martin Luther's Basic Theological Writings* (Minneapolis: Fortress Press, 1989), p. 596.

7. This is not the time and the place to unpack ethical naturalism and moral realism. Suffice it to say that I am committed to the view that there is a "there there," that there are truths to be discerned about the world, and that the world is not just so much putty in our conceptually deft hands. The world exists independent of our minds, but our minds possess the wonderful capacity to apprehend the world, up to a point, given the fallibility of reason.

8. One example would be the work of philosopher Judith Jarvis Thompson, known for her current support of physician-assisted suicide, but who first

To be sure, the freedom of a real, not a fanciful, human being means, among other things, that one can "project oneself imaginatively into a situation in which the constraints of present experience no longer hold."[9] One can strive to imagine states of perfection or nigh-perfection. At the same time, actual freedom is always situated; it is not an abstract position located nowhere in particular. Freedom is concrete, not free-floating. Freedom is a "basic human good. Life without freedom is not something we would choose, no matter how comfortable the material circumstances might be."[10] Our reasoning capacity is part and parcel of our freedom. But that reasoning is not a separate faculty cut off from our embodied selves; instead it is profoundly constituted by our embodied histories and memories.

Christian freedom, in Lovin's words, consists in our ability to "avoid excessive identification with the surrounding culture, since that tends both to lower . . . moral expectations and to deprive [persons] of the witness to alternative possibilities."[11] If the horizon lowers excessively and all is collapsed into immanence,

---

made her reputation by providing justifications for abortion by drawing an analogy between a woman hooked up during her sleep to a violinist for whom she was then required to provide life support, and a woman in relation to the fetus she is carrying. Thompson claimed that the woman would be within her rights to unhook the violinist, even if it meant his or her death; similarly, a woman is not required to carry a fetus to term. I have never understood why any reasonable person would find this argument reasonable. Fetuses do not get attached covertly but emerge as a result of action in which the woman is implicated. Moreover, the fetus's dependence on the mother for sustenance for nine months is part of the order of nature — it simply is the way humans reproduce. There are many ways to sustain violinists in need of life support, and an adult violinist is scarcely analogous in any way to the life of a human being in utero, one who is utterly dependent.

9. Robin Lovin, *Niebuhr and Christian Realism* (Cambridge: Cambridge University Press, 1995), p. 123.

10. Lovin, *Niebuhr and Christian Realism,* p. 126.

11. Lovin, *Niebuhr and Christian Realism,* p. 94.

the possibility that we might exercise our capacity for freedom is correlatively negated. So the denial of freedom consists, in part, in a refusal to accept the freedom that is the human inheritance of finite, limited creatures "whose capacities for change are also limited, and who can only bring about new situations that are also themselves particular, local, and contingent."[12] To presume more is problematic, launching us into a pridefulness that may itself be the fruit of sloth, given our cultural matrix; to presume less is to engage in a denial of finitude that helps to underwrite forms of unfreedom, often, of course, in the name of great ideals, like choice or justice. So our freedom is, at one and the same time, both real and limited.

With this as backdrop, let's examine current projects of self-overcoming that constitute examples of denial of finitude as a form of slothfulness, indolence where cultural demands and trumpeted enthusiasms are concerned.[13] These projects are tricky to get at critically because they present themselves to us in the dominant language of our culture — choice, consent, control — and because they promise an escape from the human condition into a realm of near mastery. We are readily beguiled with the promise of a new self. In so doing, we may deny or harm the only self we have. Consider, then, that we are in the throes of a

12. Lovin, *Niebuhr and Christian Realism,* p. 130.

13. This, too, is more complex than simple acquiescence. For example, where the matter of abortion — taken up below — is concerned, there is enormous popular support for some forms of restriction and restraint on the practice. The elite culture (the media, those with incomes over $50,000 per year, lawyers) long ago fell into lockstep with an absolute abortion "right," including partial-birth abortion, a practice the American Medical Association itself has declared not to be a legitimate medical procedure. So on the level of opinion all is not homogeneous. But this opinion rarely translates into action of any sort. Thus the atrophy of civic habits of the past four decades or so goes hand-in-hand with the triumph of projects that constitute flights from finitude.

structure of biological obsession that undermines recognition of both the fullness and the limitations of embodiment.[14] We are bombarded daily with the promise that nearly every human ailment or condition can be overcome if we just have will and skill enough. (Money helps, too.) As we seek cures for the human condition, the desperate edge of that seeking bespeaks a conviction that our imperfect embodiment *is* the problem that must be overcome. For example: a premise — and promise — driving the Human Genome Project, the massive effort underway to map the genetic code of the entire human race, is that we might one day intervene decisively in order to guarantee better if not perfect human products.[15] Claims made by promoters and advocates

14. Not ours alone, of course, but I will concentrate primarily on North American culture in depicting this obsession and grappling with its hold on the collective psyche.

15. Just to be clear at the outset, here I do not intend to issue strictures against any and all attempts to intervene through modern forms of gene therapy in order to forestall, say, the development of devastating, inherited conditions or diseases. There is a huge difference between preventing an undeniable harm — say a type of inherited condition that dooms a child to a short and painful life — and striving to create a perfect human specimen, one without blemishes. How one differentiates the one from the other is part of the burden of argument. One example of justifiable intervention would be a method of gene therapy that spares children "the devastating effects of a rare but deadly inherited disease. In the condition, Crigler-Najjar syndrome, a substance called bilirubin, a waste product from the destruction of worn-out red blood cells, builds up in the body. . . . Bilirubin accumulates, causing jaundice, a yellowing of the skin and the whites of the eyes. More important, bilirubin is toxic to the nervous system, and the children live in constant danger of brain damage. The only way they can survive is to spend 10 to 12 hours a day under special lights that break down the bilirubin. But as they reach their teens, the light therapy becomes less effective. Unless they can get a liver transplant, they may suffer brain damage or die." Because previous attempts at gene therapy have all fallen far short of expectations, none of this may work. But it would spare a small number of children tremendous suffering, and this sort of intervention is entirely defensive — it involves no eugenics ideology of

run to the ecstatic, for example, Walter Gilbert's 1986 pronouncement that the Humane Genome Project "is the grail of
human genetics . . . the ultimate answer to the commandment
'Know thyself.' "[16] In the genome-enthusiast camp, they are already talking about Designer Genes — that is *genes,* not jeans.
Do you want a blue-eyed, blond-haired strapping youth with
athletic tendencies, perfect teeth, and a 75-year warranty? I exaggerate but not by much. Note that an advertisement reported by
The New York Times in early spring, 1999, one that had appeared
in college newspapers all over the country, reads as follows:

EGG DONOR NEEDED
LARGE FINANCIAL INCENTIVE
INTELLIGENT, ATHLETIC EGG DONOR NEEDED/FOR
LOVING FAMILY
YOU MUST BE AT LEAST 5'10"
HAVE A 1400+ SAT SCORE
POSSESS NO MAJOR FAMILY MEDICAL ISSUES
$50,000
FREE MEDICAL SCREENING
ALL EXPENSES PAID.[17]

As *Commonweal* noted in an editorial prompted by this advertisement, it brings back eerie reminders of earlier advertisements

any kind. See Denise Grady, "At Gene Therapy's Frontier, the Amish Build a
Clinic," *The New York Times, Science Times,* Tuesday, June 29, 1999, p. D1. See
also Neil Messer, "Human Cloning and Genetic Manipulation: Some Theological and Ethical Issues," *Christian Ethics* 12, no. 2: 1-16. Messer notes the
distinction between *therapeutic* genetic intervention that involves only somatic cells, which do not play a direct role in sexual reproduction, and *non-
therapeutic* alteration of germ-line cells, which do.

16. Cited in Roger Shattuck, *Forbidden Knowledge* (New York: St. Martin's, 1996), p. 178.

17. As reprinted in an editorial in *Commonweal* 126 (26 March 1999): 5.

that involved trade in human flesh (the reference point being the slave trade) and suggests that "we are fast returning to a world where persons carry a price tag, and where the cash value of some persons . . . is far greater than that of others."[18] The *reductio ad absurdam,* at least to date, of the quest for perfection and beauty via reproductive strategies tied to selling human eggs for profit is no doubt "Ron's Angels." One Ron Harris, a fashion photographer, posted a web site in October that features models auctioning their ovarian eggs for up to $150,000. This is about 50 times more than the usual $3,000 that eggs donors are paid by fertility clinics, according to newspaper reports. The web site, pandering to another cultural fixation, is www.ronsangels.com. A veritable tangle of cultural obsessions here come together: beauty, money, guaranteed perfection in offspring, and angels hovering nearby and telling us sweetly that everything will be just fine if our intentions are good. Ethicists did rush into the breach to criticize *this* particular operation. But it is difficult for most because the weight of assessment long ago veered heavily in the direction of acceptance of donor eggs. What makes Ron's angels odious is the crassness of the operation, not the operation per se, it seems. Perhaps, then, we will say something like: 'This has gone too far. We must regulate.' But we know something even stranger and more dubious will come along and then Ron's angels will be sanitized by comparison. Sometimes there really are slippery slopes, and in this area we seem to be on one. Soberer voices — including those within the scientific community who say, "Whoa, let's slow down a bit," are drowned out by the clammering chorus of huzzahs.

After having noted that the early promises of genetic inter-

---

18. *Commonweal* editorial, p. 5. See also Margaret Talbot, "The Egg Women," *The New Republic,* 16 March 1998, 42, and Rebecca Mead, "Eggs for Sale," *New Yorker,* 9 August 1999, pp. 56-70. The latter is particularly chilling.

vention to forestall "serious health problems, such as sickle-cell anemia, cystic fibrosis, and Huntington disease," have thus far had only the meagerest success, scientist Doris T. Zallen, swimming against the cultural tide, takes up the booming genetic enterprise that promises not prevention of harm but the attainment of perfection. It is called "genetic enhancement." One starts with a healthy person and then moves to perfect. Zallen calls this the "genetic equivalent of cosmetic surgery." The aim is to make people "taller, thinner, more athletic, or more attractive." Zallen lists potential harms, including reinforcement of "irrational societal prejudices. For instance, what would happen to short people if genetic enhancement were available to increase one's height?" The "historical record is not encouraging," she adds, noting the earlier eugenics movement with their hideous outcomes, most frighteningly in Nazi Germany, but evident in this country as well, where policies of involuntary sterilization of persons with mental retardation and other measures were taken apace.[19]

IT IS important to take note of the fact that several kinds of responses to the *libido sciendi* run amok are possible, one that prevails in this text — the theological, philosophical, and ethical — but another that comes from science itself. Here the calmer voices, by contrast to promotions of the dominant and wildly optimistic sort, remind us that the scientific community at present has only the "vaguest understanding" of the details of genetic instruction — unsurprising when one considers that each "single-celled conceptus immediately after fertilisation" involves a "100-trillion-times miniaturised information system."[20] Yet the

19. Doris T. Zallen, "We Need a Moratorium on 'Genetic Enhancement,'" *The Chronicle of Higher Education,* 27 March 1998, p. A64.

20. James LeFanu, "Geneticists Are Not Gods," *The Tablet,* 12 December 1998, p. 1645.

enthusiasts who proclaim that the benefits of genetic manipulation are both unstoppable and entirely beneficial downplay any and all controversies, and short-circuit any and all difficulties, but play up complexity only so long as it works only in their favor. In this way, they can disdain any and all "nonexpert" criticism in a manner that "effectively precludes others coming to an independent judgement about the validity of their claims."[21] So we cannot have the ethical and cultural discussion we need, and those who try to promote such are seen as having joined the ranks of techno-Ludditism, including scientists who remind other scientists (as well as the beguiled public) of the thus-far insurmountable obstacles to glittering genetic transformation.

In the 1997 film *Gattaca,* not a very good film but an instructive one, the protagonist (played by Ethan Hawke) is born the "old-fashioned way" (a "faith-birth") to his parents, who had made love and taken their chances with what sort of offspring might eventuate. In this terrible new world, when a child is born an immediate genetic profile is done. Our protagonist, Vincent, is a beautiful but, it turns out, genetically hapless child (on the standards of the barren world that is to be his lot) who enters life amid not awe and hopefulness but misery and worry. His mother clutches the tiny newborn to her breast as his genetic quotient is coldly read off by the expert. "Cells tell all," the prophets of genoism intone. Because of his genetic flaws, for his was an unregulated birth, young Vincent is not covered by insurance; he does not get to go to school past a certain age; and he is doomed to menial service. He is a de-*gene*rate. Or, as the scanners immediately pronounce it, an "In-valid."

Vincent contrives a way to fool the system as he yearns to go on a one-year manned mission to some truly far-out planet. Only "Valids" — genetically correct human beings — are eligible for

21. LeFanu, "Geneticists Are Not Gods," p. 1645.

such elite tasks. So Vincent pays off a Valid for the Valid's urine, blood, saliva, and fingerprints and begins his arduous, elaborate ruse. For this is a world in which any bodily scraping — a single eyelash, a single bit of skin sloughing — might betray one. Why would a Valid sell his bodily fluids and properties? Because the Valid is now "useless," a cripple, having been paralyzed in a car accident. Indeed, his life is so useless on society's standards (that he, in turn, has thoroughly internalized) that, at the film's conclusion, and after having stored sufficient urine and blood that Vincent can fool the system for years to come, the crippled Valid manages to ease himself into a blazing furnace — to incinerate himself — life not being worth living any longer, not for one who cannot use his legs.

As for Vincent, and despite some very tense moments, life is as good as it is ever going to get by film's end: he has made love to Uma Thurman and he has faked his way (with the connivance of a sympathetic security officer) onto the mission to the really far-out planet of which he has dreamt since childhood, despite his genetically flawed condition. This is a bleak film. The only resistance Vincent can come up with is faking it. He has no language of protest and ethical distance available to him. This is just the world as he and others know it and presumably will always know it. Uma Thurman's intimacy with an "In-valid" is as close to resistance as she can get.[22] There are no alternative points of reference or resistance. Every window to transcendence has been slammed shut. It is a world no reasonable or minimally decent person would wish to inhabit.

Of course, we are not in the *Gattaca* nightmare yet. But are we drawing uncomfortably close? There are many who believe so, including the mother of a Down's syndrome child who wrote

22. A bit reminscent of Julia, the young female sexual revolutionary in Orwell's *Brave New World,* who is defeated and comes to love Big Brother.

me after she had read one of my columns about genetic engineering in *The New Republic.* I had mused, in that piece, on what our quest for bodily perfection might mean over the long run for the developmentally different. My interlocutor, whose child had died, tragically, of a critical illness in his third year, wrote me that she and her husband were enormously grateful to have had "the joyous privilege of parenting a child with Down syndrome. . . . Tommy's [not his real name] birth truly transformed our lives in ways that we will cherish forever. But how could we have known in advance that we indeed possessed the fortitude to parent a child with special needs? And who would have told us of the rich rewards?" She continued: "The function of prenatal tests, despite protestations to the contrary, is to provide parents the information necessary to assure that all pregnancies brought to term are 'normal.' I worry not only about the encouragement given to eliminating a 'whole category of persons' (the point you make), but also about the prospects for respect and treatment of children who come to be brain-damaged either through unexpected birth traumas or later accidents. And what about the pressures to which parents like myself will be subject? How could you 'choose' to burden society in this way?"

She is right. In the name of expanding choice, we are excising our definition of humanity and, along the way, a felt responsibility to create welcoming environments for all children. If we can simply declare: they made their bed (they chose to have an "abnormal" child) and now they must lie in it, this declaration takes us, as individuals and a society, off the hook. The proponents of a complex cluster of views that, by stitching together under the rubric of expanding *choice,* enhancing *control,* and extending *freedom,* aim to diminish the sphere of the "unchosen," have been enormously successful in their efforts to convince people that they are incapable of the work of care and love when it comes to a child with "special needs."

The needs of all children are special and particular, of course. The category of "special need" sprang up at one point in our recent past with concern and compassion in mind. But we have now decided, as a culture, that ordinary folks no longer possess competence in this area, thereby truncating the arena of our own free responsibility and falling into expert-sanctioned sloth. At the same time, we enlarge without limit (save whatever pragmatic cut-off points might pertain at any given moment) a notion that parents — or, more specifically, the woman, married or not — possesses absolute power of life and death over life in utero. But we shrink the domain of hands-on, everyday competence of ordinary women and men by insisting — for this is the direction "choice" takes at present — that they rid themselves of "wrongful life" in order to forestall "wrongful births" that will burden them (they will capsize under the demands) and, even more importantly, the wider society. This, in turn, makes it more difficult than ever to consider the possibility that the present abortion "right," this freedom we have embraced, often embodies a great burden for women who are told that they *alone* have the power to choose whether to have a child and that they *alone* are expected to bear the consequences if they do not choose to do so. The growing cultural conviction that children with disabilities ought never be born and that prospective parents of such children ought always to abort undermines the felt skein of care and responsibility for *all* children.[23] If we take another look at the moment when an abortion "right" got invented, it should help to make this clearer.

According to the Supreme Court, in *Roe v. Wade,* the relevant

23. Please note that I do not want in any way to diminish the difficulties involved in parenting a child with disabilities. As the mother of an adult daughter with mental retardation, I understand this very well. Instead, I am trying to capture the present temperament that dictates that such births are calamitous and ought never occur.

"decision-maker" where abortion is concerned in the first trimester is *the woman alone* or "her responsible physician." Notice the denial of relationality in the official reasoning, a denial that makes it more difficult to take notice of the occlusion of relationality and community that often brings a woman to the abortion clinic in the first place. What we should notice, and lament as a tragedy or a difficult situation, instead becomes an exemplary freedom. Sloth enters in the rapidity with which many men simply absconded in light of *Roe v. Wade:* "It's your choice, dear, it's entirely up to you." Unsurprisingly, men of the upper middle class have been the most enthusiastic supporters of an untrammeled abortion right from the very beginning. Sloth enters in our acquiescence in the sanctioned conviction that freestandingness means the right to deny the body of another in utero. Sloth enters when the *only* form Christian protest takes is to counter the abortion right with fetal rights. What about the responsibility of the Christian community to reach out to pregnant women in need of practical, hands-on assistance, the concrete form that stewardship in this area should take? We need more support in this society for mothers, fathers, and families. Instead, what we seem to get is an ever more rigid bifurcation of our discourse into a *pas de deux* between distorted views of freedom.

The heart of the matter lies in a loss of appreciation of the nature of human embodiment. The social imaginary — which the dominant scientific voices in the area of genetic engineering, technology, and "enhancement" have joined — declares the body to be a construction, something we can invent. We are loathe to grant the status of givenness to any aspect of ourselves, despite the fact that human babies are wriggling, complex, little bodies preprogrammed with all sorts of delicately calibrated reactions to the human relationships "nature" presumes will be the matrix of child nurture. If we think of bodies concretely in this way, we are then propelled to ask ourselves questions about the world little bodies enter: is it welcoming, warm, responsive? But if we tilt in the biotech constructivist direction, one in which the body is so much raw material to be worked on and worked over, the surroundings in which bodies are situated fades as The Body gets enshrined as a kind of messianic project.

The body we currently inhabit becomes the imperfect body, the one subject to chance and the vagaries of life, including illness and aging. This body has become our foe. The new body to come — extolled in manifestos, promised by enthusiasts, embraced by many ordinary citizens — is to be our gleaming fabrication. For soon, surely, we will have found a way round the fact that our poor foremothers and forefathers, living in a less enlightened era than our own, took for granted — that the body must weaken and falter and one day pass from life to death. The future perfect body will not be permitted to falter. The body may grow older in a strictly chronological sense, but why should we? So we devise multiple strategies to fend off aging. We represent aging bodies as those of teenagers with gleaming gray hair. These strategies and concerns speak to our repudiation of finitude and to our longing for full self-possession. Rather than approaching matters of life, death, and health with humility, knowing that we cannot cure the human condition, we seek cures in the assumption that the more we control the better.

Notice the similarity between this project and that which drives the marketization of everyday life discussed in chapter 2, namely, that there is nothing that is good in itself, including embodied existence. Good is reduced to a strictly consequentialist set of criteria that is up for measurement and comparison and to be adjudicated in functionalistic terms. Thus it becomes quite easy to be rather casual about devising and implementing strategies aimed at selective weeding out or destruction of the bodies of those considered imperfect or abnormal. If we are even the least bit queasy about this sort of thing, that can be at-

tributed to the lingering, residual effects of irrational or super-
stitious attitudes surrounding the human body, many sustained
by religion. Should not a concerned person raise the alarm and
ask, for example, whether, if we continue down this road, at
one point in the not-too-distant future old age might itself be
considered anomalous when measured against blooming
youth? (Or, should I say, those among the elderly who are no
longer teenagers with gray hair, hence a drag on society.) Will
the unproductive elderly at that point be encouraged, in the interest of an overall social benefit, to permit themselves to be
euthanized because they are extra mouths to feed and a nuisance to just about everybody? These sorts of questions are immediately cast as retrograde, or as part of a science fiction
dystopian mentality. For in such matters the progressivist teleology yet holds sway — that frame of mind, remember, that
would have us see only the most benign effects of change, including or perhaps especially those that come enveloped in the
shimmering mantle of scientific advance.

It is important to stress just how widely accepted the technocratic view is and how, slothfully, we are acquiescing in its premises. In a review in the *Times Literary Supplement* of four new
books on the genetic revolution, the reviewer opined matter-of-
factly that "we must inevitably start to choose our descendants."
He added that we do this now in "permitting or preventing the
birth of our own children according to their medical prognosis,
thus selecting the lives to come." So long as society does not
cramp our freedom of action, we will stay on the road of progress
and exercise sovereign choice over birth by consigning to death
those with a less than stellar potential for a life not "marred by an
excess of pain or disability."[24] Despite the horrible events associ-

24. But who defines excess? This is a soft criterion that now comes into
play for such "abnormalities" as cleft palate.

ated with the old eugenics, there are those, including molecular biologist Robert Sinsheimer, who call unabashedly for a "new eugenics." (Most, remember, try to avoid the word, one that Nazism and the notorious Supreme Court case *Buck v. Bell,* which permitted involuntary sterilization of "cretins," gave a bad name.) Sinsheimer writes: "The new eugenics would permit in principle the conversion of all the unfit to the highest genetic level."[25] In widespread adoption of prenatal screening, now regarded as simply routine, so much so that prospective parents who decline this panoply of procedures are treated as both ignorant and irresponsible; in litigation in which parents have sued on the bases of either wrongful birth or, through proxy, when the child has sued on grounds of wrongful life, we once more see the widespread presumption that life should be wiped clean of any and all imperfection, inconvenience, and risk. Creation is hobbled and bobbled. We must put it right.

The New York Times alerted us to this fact in an essay, "On Cloning Humans, 'Never' Turns Swiftly into 'Why Not,' " by

25. Quoted from the journal *Engineering and Science* in Shattuck, *Forbidden Knowledge,* pp. 193-94. The literature of reportage, enthusiasm, concern, etc., is nearly out of control. A few magazine and newspaper pieces worth reading include: Jim Yardley, "Investigators Say Embryologist Knew He Erred in Egg Mix-Up," *The New York Times,* Saturday, April 17, 1999, p. A13; Martin Lupton, "Test-tube Questions," *The Tablet,* 20 February 1999, pp. 259-60; David L. Marcus, "Mothers with Another's Eggs," *U.S. News and World Report,* April 13, 1999, pp. 42-44; Nicholas Wade, "Panel Told of Vast Benefits of Embryo Cells," *The New York Times,* Thursday, December 3, 1998, p. A24; Anne Taylor Fleming, "Why I Can't Use Someone Else's Eggs," *Newsweek,* April 12, 1999, p. 12; Nicholas Wade, "Gene Study Bolsters Hope for Treating Diseases of Aging," *The New York Times,* Friday, March 5, 1999, p. A12; Lisa Belkin, "Splice Einstein and Sammy Glick. Add a Little Magellan," *The New York Times Magazine,* 23 August 1998, pp. 26-31, 56-61, a chilling piece that shows the many ways in which geno-enthusiasm and commodification fuse; Stephanie Armour, "Could Your Genes Hold You Back?" *USA Today,* Wednesday, May 5, 1999, pp. B1-2.

their science editor, Gina Kolata.[26] Kolata points out that, in the immediate aftermath of Dolly, the cloned sheep who stared out at us fetchingly from the covers of so many newspapers and magazines, there was much consternation and negative rumbling — I recall very well, for I was one of the rumblers.[27] But opposition dissipated quickly, she continues, with fertility centers already conducting "experiments with human eggs that lay the groundwork for cloning. Moreover, the Federal Government is supporting new research on the cloning of monkeys, encouraging scientists to perfect techniques that could easily be transferred to humans." A presidential ethics commission may have recommended a "limited ban on cloning humans," but, after all, "it is an American tradition to allow people the freedom to reproduce in any way they like." Really? Since when? In any way they like? This is simply false to the historical and legal record. This society, in common with any society of which we have any knowledge, past or present, has built into its interstices a variety of limitations on "reproductive freedom." But the view that "freedom" means doing things in "any way one likes" prevails as a cultural norm. Attempts to counter such subjectivist construals tend to flounder — not because they are bad arguments, but because the tide of cultural absolutism in this matter runs so swift and so strong. Thus opposition to "any way one likes" disappears like the morning's dew at first sun.[28]

The tenor has changed, according to *The New York Times,* which describes a "slow acceptance" of the idea of cloning in the scientific community — an acceptance that took all of six

26. December 2, 1997, pp. Al, A17.

27. This foreboding also comes through in Bryan Appleyard, *Brave New Worlds: Staying Human in the Genetic Future* (New York: Viking, 1998).

28. I cannot here deal with the commercialization of genetics, but the huge amounts of profit to be made drives much of the scientific and technological work, alas. See, for example, Lisa Belkin, "Splice Einstein," pp. 26-31.

months to go from horror or queasiness to acquiescence or hearty approval. Besides, the article concludes, "some experts said the real question was not whether cloning is ethical but whether it is legal." One doctor is quoted, at article's end, in these ominous words: "The fact is that, in America, cloning may be bad but telling people how they should reproduce is worse. . . . In the end . . . America is not ruled by ethics. It is ruled by law." Law and ethics are presumed separated by a chasm, a claim contrary to the dominant Western tradition of natural law. But the implication of this view is that no mere ethical norm or standard or commitment or insight can be brought to bear whether to criticize or to checkmate statutory laws, should they be unjust or unwise. Were this day actually to arrive, it would mean that we had given up on critical politico-ethical projects, thereby diminishing our domain of free responsibility. One might call this slothful triumphalism, although this definitely sounds weird. But consider that it would mean we were not merely slothful but militantly so. Thus we would have paved additional miles on the fast track toward eradication of any real integrity to the category of "the human," and we would have displaced altogether any notion of "the natural." Law, separated definitively from ethics, would trump all.[29]

Professor Laurence Tribe of the Harvard Law School hastens to reassure us on this score. He argues thus: If we ban cloning of humans, we diminish choice, and we do so illegitimately

---

29. Think, by the way, of what this would have done to Martin Luther King's protest: simply stopped it dead in its tracks. For the law of the Jim Crow South was the law of segregation, and no ethical argument can challenge the law. End of story. A comeback would be that you need to make a legal argument to change the law. But King's call for legal change was an ethical call. The reductive argument that law and ethics must never touch is a crude form of legal positivism, or command-obedience legal theory. What is *right* does not enter into the picture at all.

by appealing to divine commandment or inspiration. This means we will automatically "criminalize" a method for "creating human babies." This blights human freedom and portends a "grave" evil, that of creating a "caste system" of the cloned. How so? Because if we ban cloning, we will make clones "a marginalized caste," so it follows that the "social costs of prohibition" are too high.[30] I thought, when I first read this piece, not having noted initially who was its author, that I was reading a parody of extreme rights absolutism. Not so, of course, once I took note of the author's name.

It is hard to imagine a stranger argument, one that makes a preemptive strike to knock down *any* and *all* possible arguments against, or barriers to, an entirely abstract and hypothetical freedom that no one can actually experience. All the heavy artillery — *choice, freedom, marginalization, forbid* — comes into play. The children of light favor this new freedom. Those who consider themselves under irrational divine sanction promote the "evil" of diminished choice and would "marginalize" clones. *They,* therefore, are the unjust, cruel children of darkness. They must be stopped before they negate an entirely abstract, hypothetical, invented freedom anyone has yet to exercise! So we are enjoined to acquiesce in a new and entirely abstract freedom and take several additional, huge strides in the direction of exploding even the merest intimation of our God-given embodiment and our call to be fruitful as God has enjoined. We relinquish the authentic freedom and responsibility that is ours in favor of an entirely abstract, ideological claim that feeds and fuels narcissistic imaginings of *radical sameness.* For one can see in the enthusiasm for cloning a real fear of the different and unpredictable, a yearning for a world of guaranteed self-replication.

30. Laurence H. Tribe, "Second Thoughts on Cloning," *The New York Times,* Friday, December 5, 1997, p. A23.

Many are those, from technology and commerce, who have rushed in to seize the title of voluptuaries of this as-yet unexercised freedom, our opposition having vanished after six arduous months of trying to hold the line. Perhaps one recalls Chicago physicist Richard Seed — an admitted entrepreneur who, nevertheless, illustrates currents at work among soberer sorts — who, in January 1998, announced that he planned to clone a human being sometime over the next year and a half. Seed claimed that God supported his endeavor because God wants us to be just like him and God gave us the power to clone. One wonders where Seed learned his theology. The Christian tradition teaches us that we are called to be co-creators, to participate in creation rather than to dominate and attain mastery over it. To seek to be identical to God is idolatry; it is perhaps the *point d'appui* of the sin of pride. For a culture to acquiesce in the march of such pride is a saddening display of the sin of sloth. As the Pontifical Academy noted in a statement on human cloning issued June 25, 1997, "Human cloning belongs to the eugenics project and is thus subject to all the ethical and juridical observations that have amply condemned it. As Hans Jonas has already written, it is 'both in method the most despotic and in aim the most slavish form of genetic manipulation; its objective is not an arbitrary modification of the hereditary material but precisely its equally arbitrary *fixation* in contrast to the dominant strategy of nature."[31]

31. Pontifical Academy for Life, "Reflections on Cloning," *Origins* 28, no. 1 (21 May 1998): 15. The popular press has been filled with articles about cloning. A few include Sheryl WuDunn, "South Korean Scientists Say They Cloned a Human Cell," *The New York Times,* Thursday, December 17, 1998, p. A12; Nicholas Wade, "Researchers Join in Effort on Cloning Repair Tissue," *New York Times,* Wednesday, May 5, 1999, p. A19; Tim Friend, "Merger Could Clone Bio-companies' Creativity," *USA Today,* Wednesday, May 5, 1999, p. 13A. See also Lori B. Andrews, *The Clone Age: Adventures in the New World of Reproductive Technology* (New York: Henry Holt, 1999).

Seed has also speculated about introducing immortality into human life, so we could all live forever "like God." But God does not "live" forever. God has no beginning or end. Seed is guilty of what Václav Havel calls "arrogant anthropocentrism" of the sort that has ravaged this century. Seed is blithely unaware of this. Even scarier, people seem to be playing along, if not with Seed's self-promoting agenda, then in "getting with the program," as we are wont to say.

We are so easily dazzled. If we *can* do it, we must do it. Better, it seems, to turn our children into objects and products. Better to risk the threat of a damaging biogenetic uniformity, since much of the basic genetic information that goes into the creation of a child from two parents emerges as a result of sexual reproduction, something not replicable by definition when one picks one parent to clone. Better to embark on an experimental course that would likely result in unused products, poor misbegotten children of our distorted imaginations, who do not quite make it to the end of the conveyor belt, as nobody wants them, not in our brave new world.[32]

32. But we have a solution to that one, too, don't we? We can be certain that the creatures nobody wants, whose lives are not "worth living," can be easily dispatched to spare their suffering. Physician-assisted suicide, the track down which we are moving, is, of course, part and parcel of the general tendencies I here discuss and criticize. Although I do not focus specifically on this matter, I recommend the following two essays for the general reader: Paul R. McHugh, "The Kevorkian Epidemic," *The American Scholar* (winter 1997): 15-27; Leon R. Kass and Nelson Lund, "Courting Death: Assisted Suicide, Doctors, and the Law," *Commentary* 102, no. 6 (December 1996): 17-29; and, as well, the late Cardinal Bernardin's "Letter to the Supreme Court," which was appended to a friend-of-the-court brief filed by the Catholic Health Association in a Supreme Court case testing the appeals of two lower court decisions that struck down laws prohibiting assisted suicide in Washington and New York states; and a brief by the U.S. Catholic Conference, "Assisted Suicide Issue Moves to Supreme Court," *Origins* 26, no. 26 (12 December 1996): 421-30.

DO I EXAGGERATE? It is hard to imagine how in light of the fantastic (and profit-making) proposals being proffered each and every day in the name of science, progress, technological control, being our own creators, and all the rest. In losing what Leon Kass calls "the wisdom of repugnance," we embark on a path that constitutes a violation of such a basic sort that it is hard to know just how to speak of it. But let me share a bit of Kass's argument before I turn to xenotransplantation as another example of the excision of the barrier of repugnance. Kass calls on us to pay close attention to what we find "offensive," "repulsive," or "distasteful," for such reactions point to deeper realities: "in this age in which everything is held to be permissible so long as it is freely done, in which our given human nature no longer commands respect, in which our bodies are regarded as mere instruments of our autonomous rational wills, repugnance may be the only voice left that speaks up to defend the central core of our humanity. Shallow are the souls that have forgotten how to shudder."[33] Kass, in other words, is arguing *for* the potential epistemic value of strong reactions, like horror at the sight of torture scenes, or revulsion when we see self-mutilation. One doesn't *end* with this reaction; nor does one discount it. Instead, Kass invites us to probe such responses since they may well gesture toward deeper realities and truths. This is *not* emotivism; it is a recognition that our responses are complex and can and should be considered.

The situation in which we find ourselves is one of sloth, acquiescence in shallow viewpoints and arguments, or so I shall characterize the gravamen of Kass's argument. For he points out that the "technical, liberal, and meliorist approaches all ignore the deeper anthropological, social and, indeed, ontological meanings of bringing forth new life. To this more fitting and pro-

33. Leon R. Kass, "The Wisdom of Repugnance," *The New Republic,* 2 June 1997, p. 20.

found point of view, cloning shows itself to be a major alteration, indeed, a major violation, of our given nature as embodied, gendered and engendering beings — and of the social relations built on this natural ground."[34] The upshot is that we cede the ground in advance of any argument having been made to the Tribes of the world, when, in fact, it should work the other way around. "The burden of moral argument must fall entirely on those who want to declare the widespread repugnances of humankind to be mere timidity or superstition."[35] But we have become slothful about defending the insights drawn from our tradition. In upending the ways we are bound and within which we are free, we do the following things, on Kass's view: we enter a world in which unethical experiments "upon the resulting child-to-be" are conducted; we deprive a cloned entity of a "distinctive identity not only because he will be in genotype and appearance identical to another human being, but, in this case, because he may also be twin to the person who is his 'father' or 'mother' — if one can still call them that"; we deliberately plan situations that we *know* — the empirical evidence is incontrovertible — are not optimal arenas for the rearing of children, namely, family fragments that deny relationality or shrink it; and we "enshrine and aggravate a profound and mischievous misunderstanding of the meaning of having children and of the parent-child relationship. . . . The child is given a genotype that has already lived. . . . Cloning is inherently despotic, for it seeks to make one's children . . . after one's own image . . . and their future according to one's will."[36]

Once the barrier of repugnance is breached, anything is possible and most things become likely. Consider xenotransplanta-

---

34. Kass, "The Wisdom of Repugnance," p. 20.
35. Kass, "The Wisdom of Repugnance," p. 21.
36. Kass, "The Wisdom of Repugnance," pp. 22-24.

tion — the transplanting of animal organs into humans — and the panoply of new experiments that accompany this particular practice. There is a hitch because, thus far, such transplantation has turned out badly; the human organism resists the pig or baboon organ. So another idea is now at work, or several. One is to perfect cloning humanlike entities — human bodies without brains — to serve as raw material for organ supplies; not having brains, they would not be human. This means we could kill them, or sustain them somehow, until we need their body parts. That not yet being perfected, there are experimenters and gene companies busy "humanizing" pigs and "pigifying" humans. This is where repugnance — a kind of aesthetic sensibility bearing ethical portents — enters. Most of us are automatically repulsed at the notion of creatures whose integrity has been radically defiled, for example, science fiction images of pig bodies with human heads attached or other bereft and forlorn creatures, like the poor, wounded, angry entities resulting from experiments on *The Island of Dr. Moreau.*

But the forces of antirepugnance are at work and this is how they work. Because no cross-species transplantation has been successful in the long term — and success is measured by the extent to which a patient has become a cellular and genetic mix of human and animal (a condition a pioneer of xenotransplantation at the University of Pittsburgh calls "post-transplantation chimerism") — moves are afoot to make such chimerism more likely. This has led to transgenesis, manipulating animals to accept genes from other species. So transgenic pigs are being raised. These are pigs that have been induced to accept human genes by injecting the female pigs' eggs with human genetic material and reimplanting them in the pig, who then gives birth to little pigs that are transgenic. These piglets are killed, and their organs are used for transplantation. The hope is that we will get more and more chimerism over time.

In a novel widely hailed as the most accomplished attempt in recent years to take the racing pulse of end-of-century (and millennium) America, Kurt Andersen puts his two protagonists — a hyped-up successful high-tech, cyber-couple named George and Lizzie (different last names) — in California (their home is New York City), where Lizzie's father has agreed to make himself available for a transgenic transplant. Enter "BAMBANG S. H. H. 'BOB' HARDIYANTI, M.D."

"Good morning. Your mother says you have several questions about our xenotransplantation protocols."

. . . "I'd like to know what we're doing to my father, yes. . . ."

"Of course," the doctor says. "We will be grafting a genetically enhanced organ from a special ungulate herd. The procedure is highly experimental, of course. As I explained to your father last evening."

"What's an ungulate herd?" Lizzie asks.

"Swine," the doctor says, smiling. "The liver was harvested from our own transgenic swine."

"You're giving my father a pig's liver?" Lizzie asks, not shocked, not horrified, just impatient at having to wade through so much euphemistic politesse.

Dr. Hardiyanti smiles a little too broadly, takes a deep breath, and nods. "Quite right. Yes. From a special herd we cosponsor. The . . . 'pigs' are genetically altered. We redesign their cells especially, you see, to trick the human immune system — your father's immune system — into accepting the liver, into letting it become *his* liver. And the liver cells are tricked, as I say, so to speak, into believing they are still living in the pig. You see? We fool the flesh, I like to say. With the goal of making each side able to live together."

Lizzie does not know if it's jet lag or Dr. Hardiyanti's pseudo-Etonian Singapore singsong, but she realizes she's taking in his explanation on two channels, like simultaneous translation. On one channel he's describing a liver transplant, but on the other he's speaking metaphorically, about some noble and terrifying scheme to engineer a global solution to racial and ethnic hate. She says nothing.

George asks, "And won't he be at risk for catching some kind of . . . pig illness?"

Dr. Hardiyanti is loving this. "These are sterile livers, I assure you. Exceptionally sterile. The piglets are removed from the womb by cesarean section. They don't suckle, they don't have any contact at all with their mothers. So they are disease free. And in a sense, they don't even know they are swine."

Lizzie is a little spooked. When will the doctor say something that isn't ripe with *Brave New World* double meaning?

[*There follows an outburst of enthusiasm from Lizzie's third or fourth stepmother, Tammy, followed, again, by words from the good doctor.*]

"We do appreciate your mother's enthusiasm," Dr. Hardiyanti says. "But I want to be quite candid. The chances of survival are, you must understand, small."

"How small?" asks George.

"Quite small."

"Like one in ten?" George asks. "One in twenty?"

The doctor says nothing.

"One in a hundred?"

"We are having real success with skin grafts from swine. And routinely for heart valves. And islets — the bits in the pancreas? At our research facility in Ventura we have a baboon that is living very successfully with a transplanted swine liver. His postop survival is now at" — Dr. Hardiyanti checks his watch — "one hundred sixty-seven days. . . . This is a wholly experimental procedure," Dr. Hardiyanti says, smiling more broadly than ever. "Wholly new. With human recipients, the success rate remains approximately zero." His beeper goes off.

"*Approximately* zero?" George and Lizzie say together in a

mixture of incredulity and curiosity that sound unpleasantly to Dr. Hardiyanti like a peer review.

Slightly taken aback, he checks his beeper message and stands. "Approaching zero, yes. In Ukraine, they claim to have a girl living for the last five months with a baby gorilla's liver. But we are, quite frankly, skeptical."[37]

Who is asking the important questions about these developments? As one critic has put it: What does it mean if "I" consist of many human and many baboon cells? If I am a mixture of different creatures, how does it affect my sense of my created integrity? (Not to mention the integrity of other creatures who cannot, by definition, put this question to themselves but can, for all that, be assaulted in their creaturely integrity.) Chimerism and transgenesis proponents — and it is a transgression of genesis that we are talking about — have no answer other than buoyant promises of living longer and maybe even forever if we get this thing perfected. Where are the limits here? Consider the origin of the term *chimera,* for the antique mythic tradition also carries warnings about breaching the barrier of repugnance. In the story of Bellerophon and his fight with the Minotaur, Bellerophon, a grandson of Sisyphus and a great tamer of horses, together with Pegasus, fights and kills the Chimera, a fearful creature that does not know what it is, being a horrible combination of lion, serpent, and goat, spitting fire from all three of its heads. Chimera is beastly because he, she, it, is a disgusting admixture of forms that do not cohere into a compelling aesthetic or ethical representation: thus all that Chimera — a perfect transgenic exemplar if

37. Kurt Andersen, *Turn of the Century* (New York: Random House, 1999). Material on transgenesis has begun to hit the popular press, where once it was the stuff of dystopian fiction. See Dan Vergano, "Of Transgenic Mice and Men," *USA Today,* Tuesday, May 25, 1999, p. 11D; Marie Woolf, "Doctors Want 'Human Pig' Transplants," *The Independent* (London), 31 January 1999, p. 1.

ever there was one — can do is to lay waste. In destroying Chimera, Bellerophon and Pegasus bring peace and safety to the people of Lycia.[38] So the warning signs have long been out. They have been there since the very inception of the Western tradition, including its pre-Christian antique form. Christians and Jews have a very specific tradition beginning with the story of a good creation by a good God. But that no longer suffices for us late moderns. We would become as gods, breach the barrier of repugnance, and, knowing not shame, create, unmindful of what is being destroyed. The great warnings no longer compute.[39]

LET US return to where we began, with the question: How far have we fallen? A burden borne by human beings after the fall lies in discerning what is natural. Can "the natural" any longer serve as a standard? The great moral teachers, until relatively recently, believed so. But we are not concerned with moral teachers in general; rather, we are engaged with what the present past of our own tradition offers. It is worth reminding ourselves at this juncture of the irreducible fact of our embodiment on the Christian understanding of our natures. We are corporeal beings. We were created as such. According to John Paul, this account — the ontological equality of male and female as corporeal beings — is "free from any trace whatsoever of subjectivism. It contains only

38. There is more to the story. Eventually Bellerophon inherits the kingdom. But his pride goes before his fall. He begins to proclaim that he is equal to Zeus. He urges Pegasus ever higher and even tries to enter Olympus. But he has flown too far. Pegasus unseats him and he plummets to earth, falling into thorns in an obscure country, compelled to wander the earth as an unknown beggar until he dies. Pegasus goes on to become the carrier of thunderbolts for Zeus. The tale is one of idealistic rapture that, if it goes too far and tries to fly, must inevitably end in a life spent in brambles and in penury.

39. See Roger Shattuck's wonderful discussion of Faust and Frankenstein in *Forbidden Knowledge,* pp. 77-107.

the objective facts and defines the objective reality, both when it speaks of man's creation, male and female, in the image of God, and when it adds a little later the words of the first blessing: 'Be fruitful and multiply and fill the earth; subdue it and have dominion over it' (Gen 1:28)."[40]

The explanation of the Genesis account figures centrally in Karol Wojtyla's prepapal writings. For example, in a series of spiritual exercises presented to Pope Paul VI, the papal household, and the cardinals and bishops of the Roman Curia during a Lenten retreat in March 1976, Karol Cardinal Wojtyla argued that "one cannot understand either Sartre or Marx without having first read and pondered very deeply the first three chapters of Genesis. These are the key to understanding the world of today, both its roots and its extremely radical — and therefore dramatic — affirmations and denials."[41] "From the beginning," in John Paul's account, is a guard against radical subjectivism; and subjectivism is "fundamentally different from subjectivity," as Wojtyla wrote in a 1960 essay on love. "Subjectivity is in the nature of love, which involves human beings, man and woman. Subjectivism, on the other hand, is a distortion of the true nature of love, a hypertrophy of the subjective element such that the objective value of love is partially or wholly swallowed up and lost in it."[42]

This subjectivism grounds what Colin E. Gunton has called "the rootless will" of late modernity that begins with an aggressive denial "of the possibility of objective meaning and truth."[43]

40. John Paul II, *Original Unity of Man and Woman: Catechesis on the Book of Genesis* (Boston: St. Paul Editions, 1981), p. 23.
41. Karol Wojtyla, *Sign of Contradiction* (New York: Seabury, 1979), p. 24.
42. Karol Wojtyla, *Love and Responsibility* (New York: Farrar, Straus, Giroux, 1981), p. 153.
43. Colin E. Gunton, *The One, the Three and the Many: God, Creation and the Culture of Modernity* (Cambridge: Cambridge University Press, 1993), p. 102.

We lose argumentation — what is there to argue about if there is no truth to be found — and "the demonstration" replaces the *disputatio*. The upshot, ironically, is "an overevaluation of the success of the scientific method and an undervaluation, if not complete relativization, of the methods of the humanities."[44] By contrast, an authentic appreciation of plurality "in the sense of a diversity of voices contending for truth" is evidence "against, not for, the postmodernist denial of objective meaning and truth."[45] For the "only *logos* underlying the postmodernist world is that of a dissipated and fragmented cultural pluralism," a world quite different from a robustly contesting plurality of voices. Gunton reiterates that the doctrine of creation is the very heart of the matter.[46] And not only because it teaches about the origin of things, about beginnings, but "as an articulation of the way things are by virtue of the relation they have with their creator."[47] Denying that relationship, we fall into subjectivism, into a world of rootless wills.

Bonhoeffer would agree. Too little has been made of Bonhoeffer's discussion of "The Natural" in his *Ethics* and of his conviction that this concept, having fallen "into discredit in Protestant ethics," had become the preserve almost exclusively of Catholic thought. Bonhoeffer aims to resurrect "the natural" and, in so doing, he draws closer to the position unpacked by John Paul II in his catechesis on Genesis. Bonhoeffer claims that fallen creation still has access to the natural, but only "on the basis of the gospel."[48] For the "natural is that which, after the Fall, is directed towards the coming of Christ." In his move to redeem

---

44. Gunton, *The One, the Three and the Many,* p. 103.
45. Gunton, *The One, the Three and the Many,* p. 105.
46. Gunton, *The One, the Three and the Many,* p. 107.
47. Gunton, *The One, the Three and the Many,* p. 124.
48. This discussion in Bonhoeffer's *Ethics* appears on pp. 142-85, and all quoted matter is drawn from those pages.

the concept of the natural, Bonhoeffer argues that we enjoy a "relative freedom" in natural life. But there are "true and . . . mistaken" uses of this freedom, and these mark "the difference between the natural and the unnatural." He throws down the gauntlet: "Destruction of the natural means destruction of life. . . . The unnatural is the enemy of life."

It is unnatural to approach life from a false "vitalism" or excessive idealism or, contrastingly, from an equally false "mechanization" and lassitude that shows "despair towards natural life," expressing as it does "a certain hostility to life, tiredness of life and incapacity for life." Our right to bodily life is a natural, not an invented, right and the basis of all other rights, given that Christian teaching repudiates the view that the body is simply a prison for the immortal soul. Harming the body harms the self at its core. "Bodilyness and human life belong inseparably together," in Bonhoeffer's words. Our bodies are ends in themselves, and this has "very far-reaching consequences for the Christian appraisal of all the problems that have to do with the life of the body, housing, food, clothing, recreation, play and sex." We can use our bodies and the bodies of others well or ill.

The most striking and radical excision of the integrity and right of natural life is "arbitrary killing," the deliberate destruction of "innocent life." Bonhoeffer notes abortion, killing defenseless prisoners or wounded men, and destroying lives we do not find worth living — a clear reference to Nazi euthanasia and genocidal policies toward the ill, the infirm, all persons with handicaps.[49] "The right to live is a matter of the essence" and not

---

49. This is an area that deserves longer treatment than I can here give it. Fortunately, and at long last, there are texts in English on Nazi euthanasia as part of its general biopolitics. Of special note is Michael Burleigh, *Death and Deliverance* (Cambridge: Cambridge University Press, 1994). This is a tremendously disquieting book for a contemporary American reader. So much of the language of our own genetic engineering and "assisted suicide" propo-

of any socially imposed or constructed values. Even "the most wretched life" is "worth living before God." Other violations of the liberty of the body include physical torture, arbitrary seizure and enslavement (American slavery is here referenced) and deportations, separation of persons from home and family — the full panoply of horrors the twentieth century has dished up in superabundance. The fragment by Bonhoeffer on the natural is unfinished — as is the entirety of his *Ethics* — but I want now to move to another of our sins of sloth that I find consistent with his argument, namely, the death penalty.

Oliver O'Donovan has recently offered up a strenuous defense of the death penalty, mounting an argument against John Paul's virtual excision of the death penalty in the encyclical "Evangelium Vitae."[50] For John Paul, "The horizon of death extends over the whole perspective of human life on earth. . . . Awareness of the meaning of the body and awareness of its generative meaning come into contact, in man, with awareness of death, the inevitable horizon of which they bear within them, so to speak."[51] The very structure of human identity embodies both the mystery of creation and the mystery of redemption: this is the fullness of an adequate theological anthropology. Because John

---

nents seems to echo National Socialist propaganda. The Nazis covered the waterfront, justifying their programs of systematic selective elimination of the "unfit," of life unworthy of life (congenitally "diseased," handicapped, etc.) on a number of interrelated grounds, including cost-benefit criteria, perfecting the race, and compassion. The Nazis also controlled the media on this issue (it goes without saying), producing short propaganda films and full-length features, lavishly produced and starring German matinee idols, to promote their euthanasian efforts.

50. Oliver O'Donovan, "The Death Penalty in *Evangelium Vitae*," in Reinhard Hutter and Theodor Dieter, eds., *Ecumenical Ventures in Ethics: Protestants Engage Pope John Paul II's Moral Encyclicals* (Grand Rapids: Eerdmans, 1997), pp. 216-36.

51. John Paul II, *Evangelium Vitae*, as printed in *Origins*, pp. 165, 167.

Paul so dignifies the body — as the gift of God and the gift of the self to another — he moves to interdict the death penalty; he wants to underscore what a punitive measure of excruciating proportions it is for an earthly power to efface a living representative of the *imago dei*.[52]

For John Paul, the primary form of social disorganization to which societies are currently subject is in the area of the spirit. In this way, the well-ordered commercial republics of the West, including our own, are morally disordered places. Thus, when John Paul eclipses the space for the death penalty, he is not, as O'Donovan claims, universalizing from the relative civic peace of "first world" countries and thereby creating a supererogatory legal requirement for those not blessed by such high levels of civic order. No, indeed, John Paul would surely say to O'Donovan and all who defend the death penalty on the grounds that it "has played a significant role in containing forces of lawlessness and upholding public order" in less organized societies than our own, that this claim is subject to empirical adjudication. And what the evidence shows is just how pervasive is a resort to summary execution and death by those with the power to undertake such actions and to cloak these actions in a patina of concern for law-abidingness. The apartheid regime did this sort of thing all the time when it was itself a giant lawlessness, an organized injustice.

Real Hobbesian states of nature are rare, and where they exist

---

52. An eloquent analysis of *Evangelium Vitae* and the death penalty is Thomas R. Rourke, "The Death Penalty in Light of the Ontology of the Person: The Significance of *Evangelium Vitae*," *Communio* 25 (fall 1998): 397-413. Rourke writes: "Having defined what it means to be a person in terms of (a) relation to others, (b) a communal 'we,' (c) the ontological presence of Christ, and (d) an integral relationship between nature and grace, we are ready to understand why John Paul II's move to narrow tightly the grounds for the application of the death penalty squares so well with a Christian understanding of the person."

the matter at issue is not the death penalty at all but harsh necessity attendant upon civil war: there is plenty of murder, plenty of death, execution aplenty. But this must be distinguished from the death penalty, which presupposes an established system of civil and criminal justice. So the pressure John Paul puts on regimes is precisely on those that already have established systems of civil and criminal law but who, slothfully, persist in seeing themselves through the lens of Hobbesian insecurities. As the foremost defender of a universal regime of human rights in the world today, John Paul defends, first of all, a fundamental right to bodily life. Thus he opposes the death penalty because it destroys human life and because it promotes and deepens the *lex talionis* as the way of human political life. With Bonhoeffer, he cedes to the state only penultimate, not ultimate, power. Claims to ultimacy and to the death penalty comport with one another. Indeed, the death penalty is part of what John Paul calls a "culture of death."

I GREW UP as part of that culture of death: death for death. I pretty much took the death penalty for granted. To be sure, it was a bit hard to square with scriptural injunctions and even harder to work out in light of the teachings of Jesus of Nazareth, but it seemed nevertheless the only appropriate punishment for the likes of Charles Starkweather and the killers of the Clutter family memorialized in Truman Capote's *In Cold Blood*. The bloody images of these murders stalked my childhood, perhaps because the killings took place not so far from my village of Timnath, Colorado (pop. 185). Starkweather, who had shot and killed more than ten people, was finally captured in Wyoming; to this day I recall the moment because the High Plains, including Colorado, were on alert worrying that Starkweather and his running companion might "come our way." Surely, I figured, communities were better off rid of such folks.

118

But there were other images, too — not just from Scripture but from the 1958 film, *I Want to Live!* for which Susan Hayward won an Academy Award for best actress. Hayward played a prostitute who had been framed for murder and sentenced to death. With her high heels and brassy manner, she was certainly not a good 4-H Club girl. But she was a mother and, unlike Starkweather, she had not actually killed anybody. The state of California put her through slow torture, one day scheduling her execution, the next day postponing it. I was haunted by the stark black-and-white image of her as she was being led into a gas chamber. But I thought the best way to reconcile these conflicting images was that killing Susan Hayward was a misapplication of the death penalty, whereas frying Starkweather was an appropriate punishment.

Then, when I was 18, I read Albert Camus's great essay "Reflections on the Guillotine," and I have never felt the same — at least not on this issue. Despite many subsequent provocations, I remain convinced by Camus, later by Bonhoeffer and John Paul, that the state cannot be the divine taker and giver of life as part of its penal powers. The state can claim for itself only a relative value, only penultimate power. According to Camus, this does not eliminate a community's right to self-defense. But where the matter at hand is crime and punishment, there are other ways to protect the community from murderous miscreants. What Camus means is that the state must not be an absolute value; it should not arrogate to itself the power to kill definitively. Camus is not moved by flabby sentiment. He develops the arguments for the death penalty and moves with surgical precision to defeat each argument on its own terms.

Deterrence? There is no evidence that the death penalty ever made a single murderer recoil; indeed, the prospect of death may exercise a tremendous fascination on the criminal mind. An edifying example of community justice? If so, why then do we hide executions from the public? Let's be clear about what is happening, Camus argues. Let us not, from slothfulness, refuse to look the thing in the face. Executions are a matter of cold premeditation. The state "kills to support a hypothesis": x number of murderers will be deterred by committing one real "administrative murder." Unlike Starkweather's bloody spree, the state's killing is meticulously planned. The condemned person is led to an antiseptic chamber, where he or she is strapped down and injected with sodium pentothal or electrocuted with 2,000 volts. Because the task is so grotesque, because we feel repugnance and shame, no one person is assigned culpability. Instead, the tasks are gingerly parceled out: one fastens arms, another legs, and so on. Camus insists, by contrast, that we make a wager on life, not on death, not from sentiment but in the name of "logic and realism." Camus knows — he wrote a thesis on Augustine, after all — that human beings are not by nature saintly. But the evil that humans do should not be compounded by administrative revenge. "Compassion," he writes, "does not exclude punishment, but it suspends the final condemnation. Compassion loathes the definitive, irreparable measure that does an injustice to mankind as a whole because of failing to take into account the wretchedness of the common condition."

Then Camus makes a move that draws him, Bonhoeffer, and John Paul together. State idolatry in our time has rushed in to take the place of faith. This explains why so many "humanists" have supported public executions — children of the Enlightenment leading the way to the "bloodstained gallows." Having killed the king, and indirectly God, humanity deifies itself and makes its own ends absolute. But we should be wary of our own designs — the sin of pride — and this wariness should also forestall the slide into the Slough of Sloth. "We know enough to say that this or that major criminal deserves hard labor for life. But we do not know enough to decree that he should be shorn of his future — in other words, of the chance we all have of making amends." The chance we all have of making amends. Christians, those who extol a doctrine of creation by a good God, are under some constraint to agree. But motivated primarily, I believe, by fear and constrained by sloth, we do not.[53] I submit that we fear our bodies, we fear their vulnerabilities, and that the cultural project of fleeing finitude not only shakes hands with a technocratic agenda, like cloning, but with a penal agenda, like doling out death. We seek perfection in one realm, definitive excision in the other. These cultural urgencies should haunt us because a society that can no longer accept bodily limits, including natality and mortality, is a society flinging itself into moral despair, not sturdy enlightenment.

Surely those who embrace a doctrine of Creation should extol the goodness and integrity of all bodies. For, as the *Book of Common Prayer* tells us: all the works of the Lord glorify, praise, and exalt the Lord. Listen to these magnificent words: hear them afresh; renew yourself in their restorative waters.

> Glorify the Lord, you angels and all powers of the Lord,
> O heavens and all waters above the heavens.
> Sun and moon and stars of the sky, glorify the Lord,
> praise him and highly exalt him for ever.

> Glorify the Lord, every shower of rain and fall of dew,
> all winds and fire and heat.
> Winter and summer, glorify the Lord,
> praise him and highly exalt him for ever.

53. I am not, of course, making the arrogant claim that those who support the death penalty are somehow not *real* Christians. My argument is that Christianity pushes away from the death penalty and that Christians are required to proffer reasons, especially when they favor the death penalty rather than the other way around.

Glorify the Lord, O chill and cold,
drops of dew and flakes of snow.
Frost and cold, ice and sleet, glorify the Lord,
praise him and highly exalt him for ever.

Glorify the Lord, O nights and days,
O shining light and enfolding dark.
Storm clouds and thunderbolts, glorify the Lord,
praise him and highly exalt him for ever.

It is an incarnational awareness that we are in danger of losing or that we, perhaps, have lost. We lose our amazement at life itself, at the glory of the natural. Sloth has clung to us and we cannot exalt the Lord any longer; instead, we worship at the altar of our own projects. In this regard I recommend P. D. James's novel, *The Children of Men*. The novel is set in Britain in the year 2021. No children have been born — none at all — on planet Earth since the year 1995. In that year, for reasons no one understands, all males became infertile. The world is dying. People are despondent, chagrined, violent. "Western science had been our god," writes the protagonist, Theodore Faron, an Oxford historian and cousin to the dictator of Great Britain. He "shares the disillusionment" of one whose god has died. Now overtaken by a "universal negativism," the human race lurches toward its certain demise. Because there will be no future, "all the pleasures of the mind and senses sometimes seem . . . no more than pathetic and crumbling defences shored up against our ruins." Children's playgrounds are dismantled. People disown commitments and responsibilities for one another save for whatever serves some immediate purpose: what is chosen by contrast to what is given.

People thought they had eliminated evil, Faron notes, and all the churches in the 1990s "moved from the theology of sin and redemption" to a "sentimental humanism." In the name of compassion, the elderly, no longer needed or wanted, are conducted to a state-sponsored ceremony of group suicide called the Quietus. Faron concludes that we are "diminished," we humans, if we live without knowledge of the past and without hope of the future. For in a world in which birth has ceased and death is managed and staged, "the very words 'justice,' 'compassion,' 'society,' 'struggle,' 'evil,' would be unheard echoes on an empty air." To be sure, we can "experience nothing but the present moment," but our understanding of that moment is profoundly shaped and given meaning by our "ability to reach back through the centuries for the reassurance of our ancestry." This rich ancestry loses its meaning, in turn, "without the hope of posterity . . . without the assurance that we being dead yet live." For whom do we build? In whose behalf do we dream? If we are wrapped up in our own quest for self-possession, perfection, and control, if we are immersed in the fixed immanence of our culture, we cannot even ask such questions, much less answer them.

ASPEN GROVE IN AUTUMN SNOW

Above treeline, the mountain is streaked
gray-white by snowfall fallen this year
before even half the leaves, which lie like green
and yellow coins on a white blanket. In an aspen
grove, I am amazed at the sun-glitter trembling
against a western-blue sky and the snow's sequined
surface pocked by leaves warm enough even in death
to melt drills of air through the white powder.
Light is slanting in late afternoon to an amber music,
an intermittent music, like the hiss of trains at a station,
the leaf-whispers rushing as the breeze picks up,
rushing again like surf, like something else
just thought of to say, so many goodbyes
repeated, so many reassurances
before the long parting.

FRED DINGS,
from *After the Solstice*
(reprinted with permission of the author)

Conclusion

Living in Hope

What does it mean to live in hope? Reaching a new millennium, rather like what Samuel Johnson is said to have remarked about hanging, concentrates the mind wonderfully. We take stock. We look back in order to peer ahead. We ask ourselves: Do we dare to hope, having looked back, having surveyed the shipwreck that is so much of the twentieth century? Taking stock honestly and forthrightly, refusing to avert our eyes, it is clear that optimism isn't warranted. But then, optimism never is. Hope, however, is something else. While optimism proffers guarantees that everything will turn out all right and that all problems are solvable, hope, that great theological virtue, urges us to a different stance, one aware of human sin and shortcoming but aware also of our capacities for stewardship and decency and our openness to grace. Citizens entering the twenty-first century can find reasons to hope, and those who call themselves "Christian" are claimed by hope. How can hope help to sustain critical and constructive civic projects and identities that promote our collective well-being as a people, whether one is claimed by the name "Christian" or not?

The first concrete project for citizens who live in hope is to insist that we name things accurately and appropriately. Why is this so vital? One extraordinary sign of our times is a process of radical alteration in language, understanding, and meaning. Of course, many changes in language are not only benign but embody a linguistic advance in that our descriptive powers are enhanced and our capacity to pierce closer to the reality of that which we would understand is expanded. But, on the other side, we are painfully aware of what happened when totalitarian regimes had the power to control language and to cover mass murder with the rhetoric of "improvement of the race" and even "mercy and compassion." We are much less attuned to the ways in which our own language, hence our understanding of the world, may be contorted by drawing us away from, rather than closer to, that which we are depicting.

Consider, for example, appropriation of the word *community* by enthusiasts of cyberspace.[1] "Community" derives from the Latin *communis,* from which "communion," "communicate," even the reigning image of the person in Christian anthropology as one born *in communio,* all usher. Community is grounded, concrete, tactile, relational, fleshly, or at least it must begin in this concrete way and, in principle, be open to such instantiation. It implicates us in a world of others who bind us to them as well as to a time and place. In 1938, as the world was collapsing and turning vicious all round him, Dietrich Bonhoeffer penned an urgent work, *Life Together.*[2] In this text, he meditated on the nature of a Christian community, having in mind his own

1. I am not here referring to those who regard the internet as a complex tool for research or as a way of quickly sending out functional messages; rather, I have in mind those who have become publicists of cyber-reality and who debunk the puny stuff of what most of us know as the "real world."

2. Dietrich Bonhoeffer, *Life Together: Prayerbook of the Bible,* Dietrich Bonhoeffer Works 5, trans. Daniel W. Bloesch and James H. Burtness (Minneapolis: Fortress Press, 1996).

Finkenwalde experiment where he and his seminarians shared a life together as pastors and pastors-in-becoming of the Confessing Church before the Gestapo forced the closing of their community. Community cannot exist without the physical presence of others, Bonhoeffer argued. Why? Because: "A human being is created as a body; the Son of God appeared on earth in the body for our sake and was raised in the body. In the sacrament the believer receives the Lord Christ in the body, and the resurrection of the dead will bring about the perfected community of God's spiritual-physical creatures."[3]

Scripture rightly uses the metaphor of a body — the body of Christ — to describe the church.[4] Luther describes the church not as the "wood and stone" that go into the structure but as "the assembly of people who believe in Christ. With this church one should be connected and see how the people believe, live, and teach."[5] Bonhoeffer goes on to attack all spurious forms of idealism that would have us live in psychic "reality" or in "a dream world . . . and to abandon ourselves to those blissful experiences and exalted moods that sweep over us like a way of rapture. For God is not a God of emotionalism, but the God of truth."[6] Wishful dreaming makes us "proud and pretentious." But no "visionary ideal" ever binds people together. The Christian community is "not an ideal we have to realize, but rather a reality created by

3. Bonhoeffer, *Life Together,* p. 29.

4. An interesting discussion of "The Ecclesiology of John Paul II," by Fr. Avery Dulles, S.J., appears in *Origins* 28, no. 44 (22 April 1999): 759-63. Fr. Dulles points out that John Paul's preferred category for ecclesiology is communion and that this communion is the "integrating aspect, indeed the central content of the 'mystery' or rather, the divine plan for the salvation of humanity" (p. 759).

5. Martin Luther, "The Gospel for the Early Christmas Service, Luke 2:[15-20]" (trans. J. G. Kunstmam), in *Luther's Works,* vol. 52: *Sermons II,* ed. Jaroslav Pelikan (Philadelphia: Fortress Press, 1955), pp. 39-40.

6. Luther, "Gospel for the Early Christmas Service," p. 35.

God in Christ in which we may participate."[7] Real community is mediated as we are stirred to love of neighbor through shared love in and through Christ. This actual community never excludes "the weak and insignificant, the seemingly useless people, from everyday Christian life in community," no, for "in the poor sister or brother, Christ is knocking at the door."[8] These lessons in concrete embodied community, Bonhoeffer credits to the people of Israel and their experience as handed down to us in Scripture. Further, he had picked up something of the rhythms and flow of communal monastic life given his visits to Rome and his stay in a monastery for a period.

By contrast to the concrete, nitty-gritty tactile nature of real community, think of so-called cyber-community and that "reality" called virtual. This is a form of gnosticism that is parasitic upon the concrete realities thoroughgoing cyberites disdain, with their labeling of people who are not totally hived or caught in the web as PONAs (people of no account). Writes Mark Slouka: "Already, we are told, technological prostheses had begun to 'liberate' us from the limitations of the human body. The possibilities were endless. Within the span of our children's lifetimes, we were assured, it would be possible to link the human nervous system directly to a computer, to download the human consciousness into RAM (random access memory), effectively preserving it in some artificial state. Within the foreseeable future, the dividing line between nature and technology — a false dichotomy, we were told, since at least the invention of agriculture — would be erased; genetic engineering in general, and the Human Genome Project in particular, had already blurred the line forever."[9] Divorced from our bodies, so the scenario runs, all

7. Luther, "Gospel for the Early Christmas Service," p. 38.
8. Luther, "Gospel for the Early Christmas Service," p. 46.
9. Mark Slouka, *War of the Worlds* (New York: Basic Books, 1995), pp. 18-19.

boundaries between self, other, male, female, anything and everything would disappear. We could be anyone we want. We could go anywhere we want. We could do anything we want. Reality would lose all meaning, Slouka argues. And so, I submit, would, and does, community when it takes place in cyberspace and involves no concrete, living relations of human bodies one to another, or the possibility of such. Disdain for the limitations of the natural world, including our own physicality, skyrockets. If we embrace this distention with its obliteration of any concrete reference points, we have an image of relativistic ephemera: all that is solid melts into air and we then take the air for the thing itself. This is a form of techno-gnosticism: all is spirit, intellection. Bodies matter not. Yet there is a desire to appropriate concrete words as a kind of mimetic imperative.

ONE OF America's leading social scientists, James Q. Wilson, propounded several decades ago what has become reigning wisdom among those concerned to combat violent crime and deterioration in our cities, namely, that if we decide the little things — like graffiti on all subways or buses or unrepaired chinks out of sidewalks or a bit of litter here and there — do not really matter and we let these slide, it makes it easier for the big things — brazen assaults on persons in broad daylight — to emerge and take hold. Why? Because letting the little things go, ignoring the beginnings of deterioration and decrepitude, is a sign that we no longer care about this place; we do not mind if people start to trash it. This has an insidious effect on our hearts and minds. We are dragged down and some are drawn into the process of active destruction.

I have seen this happen. At a large state university where I once taught, a place plagued by years of underfunding, maintenance slid and the infrastructure started to fray about the edges.

131

Blackboards hung askew here and there. Floors in classrooms stayed dirty. Sidewalks went unrepaired. Trash bins were not emptied frequently enough. The overall social and ethical environment began to show the signs of wear and tear. It was utterly unsurprising to me that kids on weekends and in general liked to tear up the place. It was as if they were saying: The adults responsible for this campus don't seem to mind if it goes to hell, so why should we care?

The deterioration, manipulation, and distortion of language works in a similar fashion. Once one acquiesces in euphemisms like "pacification" for harrying and hounding peasants, destroying and looting their homes, and forcing them to become desperate refugees; or "compassion" for killing helpless, imperfect human beings; or "choice" for a nigh-unlimited "right" to withdraw the boundary of moral concern from unborn children at any stage of fetal development; or "liberation" as our freedom *from* any socially or ethically sanctioned relations or commitments; or "community" for signs in cyberspace, one is on a fast track to the radical loss of meaning that so characterizes our age.

What does it mean to *name* things correctly? It does *not* mean embracing a simplistic designativist account of language and meaning, nor does it commit one to a correspondence theory of truth. Rather, I am simply urging us to pay more attention to the ways in which the abuse of language creeps up stealthily on cat's paws and may insinuate itself unawares. We think to ourselves: "that's no big deal, let them call cyberspace 'community.'" Then, when we get into a discussion of these matters, we are accused of being retrograde sticks-in-the-mud if we insist that community absent concrete relations between persons — or the possibility of such or a prior history of such — is an incoherent idea that radically dissociates the word from its multiple yet bound associations with the fellowship, not of abstract entities, but of fleshly ones.

132

One area in which the meaning of a potent term has been hotly disputed is that of the family. Those of us who, over the past three decades, insisted that it makes mincemeat of this concept to apply it to any random collection of human beings that happen to occupy a domicile at a given point in time — to refer, therefore, to persons who may have no legal, blood, deep affectionate and friendship ties to one another — were scored as being against progress and change and inclusiveness and all the rest. But "family" means something: it requires relationships that bind us in certain ways. If we stretch the term beyond recognition, we in effect carry out on linguistic terrain — which is always also ethical and political terrain — a project analogous to those flights from finitude I assayed in Chapters Two and Three above.

LIVING IN HOPE means being attuned to the ways in which language simultaneously frees us and binds us. It means *paying attention.* Those who aim to unloose language entirely from coherent tethering diminish, in doing so, the potent role of language in constituting and structuring human relations in ways befitting the complexity of persons as creators and creatures. There is a structure of human hope even as there are structures of all other complex human possibilities. Hopelessness is one by-product when meanings spiral out of control. When words implode, so do worlds. In his great work on *The Peloponnesian War,* Thucydides ties the loss of clear meanings of words to Athens's subsequent degradation and decline. He clearly intends this as a civic object lesson: beware when words lose their meaning.[10]

Words and their meanings are connected to debates about truth. The deformation of language characteristic of totalitarian regimes was an integral feature of their playing fast and loose

10. Thucydides, *The Peloponnesian War* (London: Penguin, 1982).

with facts and undermining, thereby, any possibility of shared truth-claims as a feature of political and personal life. People disappeared from photographs, were written out of history. Events were obliterated or invented. Those of us who never experienced such horrors underestimate how important truth is to people who lived for years within a tissue of state-sponsored lies.[11] This came home to me at a conference in Prague on "Truth and Politics" in 1994 at which philosophers from Central Eastern Europe, who had fought the good fight against totalitarianism, expressed their perplexity at the blithe attitude evinced by many Western philosophers concerning the question of truth.

My paper on that occasion consisted of an analysis of Hannah Arendt's complex reflections on this topic. Arendt, one of the premier political thinkers of this century, had insisted that the political world is utterly dependent on facts, for life in the plural must tend to "factual truth." Arendt argued that there is such a thing as a historical record and that we are not permitted to "rearrange the facts" in order that they might better comport with our own perspective. She cites French premier Clemenceau, who, when asked what future generations would say about responsibility for the outbreak of the First World War, replied that he was not sure how that question would finally be ironed out. "But I know for certain that they will not say Belgium invaded Germany."[12]

11. Americans are always rightly shocked to learn that their government or leaders have played fast and loose with the truth. But we have truth as a reference point. People aren't airbrushed out, made to disappear without a trace. Because the communist state, by contrast, controlled everything, one had no independent access to sources of information other than the state, if one was unlucky enough to spend forty years or more under a communist *nomenklatura*. Those who did actively search out the truth did so at great risk.

12. See Hanneh Arendt, "Truth and Politics," in *Between Past and Future* (New York: Viking, 1966), pp. 227-64, quotation at p. 239. I concentrate on this essay by Arendt, though her views appear at various places in her work.

This stubborn fact — "brutally elementary data" Arendt calls it — should remain; but if it is destroyed much more will have been lost than this one forlorn fact. For at the sad moment when a power monopoly can eliminate from the record "the fact that on the night of August 4, 1914, German troops crossed the frontier of Belgium," at that moment "power interests" will have utterly shut down a public world of freedom depending on the stubborn reality of certain humble truths. The fragility Arendt alludes to is not so much that factual truths can be ignored or suppressed but, rather, the epistemological claim that factual truths are pretty much up for grabs, almost wholly subjectivist, in the scheme of things Arendt analyzes and laments. Factual truth, for Arendt, "is always related to other people, it concerns events and circumstances in which many are involved; it is established by witnesses and depends upon testimony; it exists only to the extent that it is spoken about, even if it occurs in the domain of privacy."[13]

Bonhoeffer contributed to a discussion of truth in a controversial essay, "What Is Meant by 'Telling the Truth.'" The essay was prompted, in part, by Bonhoeffer's anguish over the deception of which he was part as a member of the anti-Nazi resistance. As a framing feature of his argument, Bonhoeffer goes after Kant in severe terms, the Kant who argued that one must tell the truth to a murderer who has come to the door looking for one's friend, who is hidden on the premises, and whom the murderer aims to kill.[14] For Bonhoeffer, this makes of the truth teller a "fanatical devotee of truth who can make no allowance for hu-

---

13. Arendt, "Truth and Politics," p. 238.

14. This is not the time to debate whether Bonhoeffer got Kant right, so to speak. Certainly, a kind of ruthless edge to ethical determination is part and parcel of strong deontological theories. And Bonhoeffer is part of the wave of philosophical and theological reasoning discontent with the so-called epistemological turn of which Kant is the giant figure.

man weaknesses; but, in fact, he is destroying the living truth between men."[15] The truth, that is, of friendship and loyalty and courage.

But Bonhoeffer is no situationist. He is not a means-end thinker who believes "the truth" can be cut and trimmed to suit our immediate political purposes; rather, what he aims to do is to preserve the preconditions within which factual truth can be recognized, a world in which its coercive force can be felt and made part of the clash of views central to politics. But if one lives in a world in which those preconditions have been utterly destroyed — and betraying a friend to a murderer aids and abets such destruction — then the most important task is to "discern the real," in Bonhoeffer's phrase, meaning that one must evaluate "what is to come" in an unflinching way and act accordingly. Bonhoeffer calls for respecting the boundaries of realities of the multiple institutions of social life — family, church, school, politics.

Bonhoeffer gives an example: a zealous teacher asks "a child in front of the class whether it is true that his father often comes home drunk. It is true, but the child denies it." The child denies it because to admit it is to expose his family to the interference of a zealous do-gooder. "The child's answer can be called a lie; yet this lie contains more truth, that is to say, it is more in accordance with reality than would have been the case if the child had betrayed his father's weakness in front of the class." The fault here is the teacher's and his or her illegitimate prying in a public setting, not the child's. "Since the term lie is quite properly understood as meaning something which is quite simply and utterly wrong, it is perhaps unwise to generalize and extend the use of this term so that it can be applied to every statement which is formally untrue." What Bonhoeffer is doing is alerting us to context and occasion — something quite different from the arbitrariness

15. This essay appears in his *Ethics*.

inherent in the view (associated with the work of philosopher Richard Rorty) that anything and everything can be redescribed and there is no truth to be found.

Arendt would be sympathetic to Bonhoeffer's case and claim. Truth and falsehood give us our "bearings in the real world." Each is contingent in one sense, namely, that things "could . . . have been otherwise." But once things have happened they cannot be undone. The systematic attempt to falsify the past is what is deadly — not the fib of a child seeking to protect himself and his father. The problem with many energetic "redescribers" is that they treat the past as if it were the future — a realm of potentiality — and, in so doing, deprive the political realm of one of "its main stabilizing force[s]." That which is new emerges out of a ground of the "already happened." If we treat the past as if it were up for grabs, depending on who had the power to redescribe, we create a cynical world in which violence can destroy truth. It is my sober assessment that the considerations Arendt evokes are becoming more difficult to articulate because we have to a large extent succumbed to the view that truth and falsehood are meaningless in the political realm and that a "peculiar kind of cynicism," defined by Arendt as "an absolute refusal to believe in the truth of anything, no matter how well this truth may be established," is widespread if not yet utterly triumphant.[16]

NOW LET'S TURN to a second claim on those who live in truth, namely, *to be prepared to offer a reasoned defense of one's position and to engage interlocutors from a stance of preparedness and openness tethered to an insistence that there is some truth to be found.* Now more than ever, Christians as citizens must be de-

16. Arendt, "Truth and Politics," p. 257.

fenders of human reason, insistent that epistemological questions cannot be severed from ontological concerns if the complexity of truth is to be approached.

Unsurprisingly, John Paul II, who shares Augustine's insistence that God's righteousness and human righteousness are linked and that this linkage extends to our capacity, in freedom, to seek the truth, taps the love of wisdom and desire for the truth that he takes as part of our very constitution. There is, he claims in the encyclical "Fides et Ratio," a kind of epistemic urgency characteristic of human beings.[17] Our sense of wonder is awakened by contemplation of creation. The danger here is that this epistemological quest may usher in what John Paul calls "philosophical pride" as we take but one stream of thought for the whole. But, at their best, our searches strengthen our capacities as "free and intelligent" subjects who have the "capacity to know God, truth and goodness." This is an extraordinary gift that should not be squandered. The church, John Paul reminds us, sets great value on reason's drive to attain goals that render people's lives more worthwhile: the church has no quarrel with the natural sciences and the other great disciplines as a matter of principle. The quarrel comes when one way of knowing comes to be taken for the whole — as, for example, the economism I assayed in Chapter Two — or when an entire approach begins from an anthropology that, if generalized as the whole truth about human beings, distorts profoundly anthropology and cannot, therefore, help to forge the epistemology-ontology link John Paul claims we cannot do without.

Continuing, John Paul reasons that a too simple fideism fails to recognize the importance of rational knowledge and philosophical discourse for an understanding of the faith. By contrast, ardent philosophical overreach denies the specific tasks of theol-

17. "Fides et Ratio," in *Origins* 28, no. 19 (22 October 1998): 319-47.

ogy in claiming that we can, we must, and indeed we have eliminated the presupposition of transcendence and slammed shut the door on those truths "available to us through grace and faith." These truths constitute beliefs that are the stuff of faith — thinking faith — for to believe is to "think with assent." John Paul then gestures toward one of the "most significant aspects of the present," namely, the "crisis of meaning" to which I have already referred. This crisis consists of radical doubt that throws us into nihilism, the triumph of instrumental thinking, a rejection of the "sapiential dimension as a search for the meaning of life," and the sheer "fragmentation of knowledge" itself. Meaning is sustained only if philosophy keeps open a "genuinely metaphysical range" that opens up before us "in truth, in beauty, in moral values, in other persons, in being itself, in God." John Paul frets throughout *Fides et Ratio* about contemporary anti-intellectualism, whether in the church or not. If anti-intellectualism and simplistic fideism are not the problem, the pridefulness of philosophical totalizers and systematizers is likely to be. In the eloquence of John Paul's argument in behalf of reason, one finds a display of robust Christian hope — that human beings might think, believe, and act in ways that are generous and large-hearted.

We are at a rather interesting moment in philosophical discourse. The so-called epistemological turn, associated with Kant, could not indefinitely hold at bay certain ontological questions. In other words, we have learned that a philosophy of consciousness cannot do without a philosophy of being, however tacit. At the same time, the so-called language turn appears to have reached a dead end when everything in the world gets turned into an arbitrary text that could as well have been anything else — when realism (in any version) is abandoned in favor of radical constructivism. This seems to be where modern reason has led us. One can detect the will-to-power lurking in the interstices of radical constructivism, a project that recognizes no intrinsic limits to what human beings can or should do, be, or become.

By contrast, when John Paul notes that Anselm "underscores the fact that the intellect must seek that which it loves. The more it loves the more it desires to know," he locks horns with one strand of modern reason, the belief that reason unaided can lead us to wisdom — though wisdom is not much sought after anymore — can lead us, perhaps better put, in current parlance, to instrumentally useful knowledge. If Christians need philosophy, philosophy needs love and illumination by faith. Otherwise the person is drawn to forms of modern reason that "lured people into believing that they are their own absolute master, able to decide their own destiny and future in complete autonomy, trusting only in themselves and their own powers." It is unsurprising that a crisis of meaning slowly but surely eventuates given this sacralization of reason. It is as if Hegel's dialectic of reason's cunning has collapsed in on itself, as any totalizing-immanent project must. What remains politically is the triumph of a form of state sovereignty that readily becomes state idolatry — one of the modern gods — in a process characterized by Albert Camus as "the vision of a history without any kind of transcendence, dedicated to perpetual strife and to the struggle of wills bent on seizing power."[18]

For Hegel, Christ is but a stage "on the road to the universal: He too must be denied dialectically. It is only necessary to recognize Him as the man-God to obtain a higher synthesis — this synthesis, after being incarnated in the Church and in Reason, culminates in the absolute State."[19] The divinizing of history and humanity leads

---

18. Albert Camus, *The Rebel,* trans. A. Bower (New York: Knopf, 1954), p. 135.

19. Camus, *The Rebel,* p. 141.

not to human liberation but to destruction. The world, if transformed into a messianic project, is terrifying, dead, even demonic. Humans cannot fulfill the terms of their self-sanctification and grow restless and empty, no matter how fast they run, how much money they make. Camus's chilling comment on the culmination of the Hegelian project with its absolutization of immanence is that: "The sky is empty, the earth delivered into the hands of power without principle."[20] Christian hope, by contrast, enlivens reason, refreshes it with the clear, at times rushing waters of joy and living witness and action. The world is not dead — it lives. We are alive to its wonder. We sing our hymns of praise. We reach toward the "splendor of the truth" insistently but with that humility befitting creatures such as ourselves.

Consider one scholarly example of wonderment at the world and all its "stuff": the work of dinosaur paleontologists. Why would a "sensible" (on the world's terms) human being set about such arduous tasks — spending hours, days, months under grueling conditions, in hot sun or pouring rain or through bitter winds and sandstorms, in order to sift painstakingly through tons of dirt and sand a teaspoon at a time looking for bone fragments, no matter how small, of creatures who have been extinct for 60 to 75 million years? There is no instrumental value here. There is instead a wonderment at the presence on our planet of extraordinary creatures whose reign lasted over 120 million years. The paleontologist wants to "get it right," to figure out when, where, and how dinosaurs — the hundreds and hundreds of different known species — lived and died. They want to bring dinosaurs back to life, to represent them among us. This is not a project driven by deadness.[21] It may turn on "bones, dem bones,

---

20. Camus, *The Rebel,* p. 148.
21. Another grandparenting benefit is reacquaintance with dinosaurs. One is apprised immediately of the extraordinary explosion of dinosaur

dem dry bones," but the work is lush with liveliness and hope and keen recognition of God's (or nature's) good humor. Dinosaurologists never lost their childlike wonderment and curiosity. Nor should any of us. "The world is so full of a number of things/I'm sure we should all be as happy as kings." But we are not. And the misuse, overextension, or atrophy of reason is at the heart of the matter.

Living in hope: reason, argue, explore joyfully. This is the only way we can come to know one another. As Francis Cardinal George proclaimed in his installation homily as Chicago's archbishop: "What the church brings to any society or neighborhood is the experience of making differences public so that they can be shared to create a richer unity. In the church every racial and cultural difference must be made public so that everyone can come to know how Christ can be black or white or brown or yellow or red. If I do not know any Mexicans or Russians or Africans or Chicagoans, I cannot experience how Christ can be Mexican or Russian or African or Chicagoan. The differences must be made public, but always in a way that they can be shared, so that they can enrich everyone."[22] This process is the work of reason in faith and love.

WE ARE NOW brought to the third, and related, difference that those who call themselves Christian can and should make in order to roll back the scrim of modern meaninglessness, and that is *to display what incarnational being-in-the-world is all about*. We are called to cultivate citizens who make visible before the world

knowledge over the past several decades. Special thanks to my colleague at the University of Chicago, Paul Sereno, who loves dinosaurs and loves to bring them to children.

22. Francis Cardinal George, "What the Church Brings to the Neighborhood," *Origins* 27, no. 1 (27 May 1997): 3.

the fullness, dignity, and wonder of creation — and horror, then, at its wanton destruction. This sounds terribly mysterious, but it is not. Modern deadness is all around us — the conviction that the world is so much matter to manipulate; that abstract signs and symbols entirely of our own creation that can be sent whirring round the globe in milliseconds are the reality that counts; and that individuation as a kind of radical aloneness simply is the human condition. We can voluntaristically try to do something about this, but we have been told that the world is intrinsically arelational. No wonder so many despair or seek solutions to a perceived sense of nonbeing in acts of violence that promise at least momentary self-transcendence. If the only "reality" is inside our own skins or heads, or the concatenated effects of our most dizzying fabrications, and the ultimate arbiter is the subjective standpoint of the one, the result is the deal that Charles Taylor calls "rotten" — a combination of crass objectivism and runaway subjectivism.

Christianity, by contrast, is a remarkably enfleshed way of being. The body is no mere container for the soul but our very essence. We are not *individuals* whose sociality is the result of voluntaristic motion but *persons* whose sociality is given. Kenneth L. Schmitz calls the notion of the person "extravagant," even lush, here remarking on the trinitarian Godhead. This trinitarian model is one that is to be "imitated and a reality to be participated in, a new sense of intimacy [that] shaped bonds between human individuals."[23] As humans moved into modernity, the transcendent dimension of this complex concept that fused together dignity, intimacy, relationality, interiority, and other features of persons began to fade. Unsurprisingly, by the seventeenth century the dominant metaphor for political organization

23. Kenneth L. Schmitz, "Reconstruction of the Person: A Meditation of the Meaning of Personality," *Crisis* (April 1999): 28.

had shifted from anything suggestive of the corporate to every-thing generated by contract. Colin Gunton argues that the pre-supposition underlying social contract theorizing is that: "Social existence is not essential to our being as humans, but a more or less unfortunate necessity. . . . Both Hobbes and Locke found their concepts of the social contract on a deficient sociality, a fail-ure to consider the essentially social nature of human being."[24] This contract metaphor implicates us in a contraction of person-hood, and the only "value" or "dignity" we have is what the con-tract permits and what nowadays the market will bear.

The signs of the times are not good in this regard; yet . . . we are haunted, haunted as the amputee is said to be of a missing limb. Our excised sociality follows us about as a kind of phantom yearn-ing to be manifest. But modern individualism dictates that this phantom self remain but a phantom. So we jauntily race about, a bit spooked from time to time, but busily self-actualizing. Then the inevitable happens. An accident, an illness, an upheaval, death. Whoa . . . what's going on here? What are these feelings about? Where do they come from? We turn to New Age sentimen-talism or drugs or drink or incessant TV but that only exacerbates our haunting, layering it over with a patina that oozes good feeling — we must get happy, happy, happy and not get hung up. *Whatever.* The tactile here-ness and this-ness of selves-in-relation — that is what contemporary forms of insistence, and our language itself, have a hard time recognizing and naming properly. Clearly, the issue of naming as a way to get us closer to the thing-in-itself is part and parcel of the embrace of incarnational reality. All these wonderful complexities and the special form Christian under-standing and witness afford us are woven together.

24. Colin E. Gunton, *The One, The Three and the Many: God, Creation and the Culture of Modernity* (Cambridge: Cambridge University Press, 1993), p. 220.

What are some concrete instances of the bleeding away of incarnate reasoning and being and, by contrast, examples of words made flesh?[25] In Chapters Two and Three I assayed both the theory and the practice of those forms of socioeconomic and cultural gnosticism in excessive commodification of the world and all that is in it and in turning the "stuff" of human being-hood into raw material to be reformed, reshaped, altered on our wills. There is no need to offer a reprise here. But revisiting contemporary flight from finitude in our approach to death and to the dying must detain us for a moment or two.

It was no doubt bound to happen, but the language — a "right" to die — despite its pervasive use, should retain the capacity to startle us. People die. One scarcely needs a right to do that. But the "right"-to-die enthusiasts claim a legal right to an "easeful" death. Architect of much of the current hoopla surrounding the issue is self-promoting pathologist Jack Kevorkian, who rails against any and all who refuse to take on board his insistence that people should have the "right" to kill themselves, and to have medical assistance in doing so, whenever they see fit. This is but one among a cluster of views he holds. Others include the right to experiment on convicted murderers before their executions — they are going to be killed anyway, so why preserve any integrity to their bodies before execution — and, as well, he has in print "excused Nazi doctors for having experimented in death camps, because at least some physiological knowledge emerged thereby from the general slaughter."[26] Kevorkian's

25. A tremendously complex discussion is Josef Seifert, *Back to 'Things in Themselves': A Phenomenological Foundation for Classical Realism* (New York/London: Routledge and Kegan Paul, 1987), especially Part II: "Objective knowledge of 'things in themselves'; constituted, unconstituted, and unconstitutable being."

26. Anthony Daniels, "A Bit of His Own Medicine," *The Independent on Sunday,* 29 November 1998, p. 30. This is an extensive and sober piece in a

"philosophy," if such a crackpot mélange of bone-chilling opinions can possibly be said to constitute such, is the most crude utilitarianism imaginable. As Anthony Daniels notes: "Assisted suicide and euthanasia are but stalking horses for Kevorkian's wider social vision of routine experimentation upon dying people and walk-in municipal suicide centres where the ill and merely disgruntled will be helped (at public expense) to shuffle off this mortal coil. They will be manned by salaried specialists in death called obitriatists, who practice patholysis, the dissolution of all suffering."[27]

Now Kevorkian would not have gotten as far as he did, or gotten away with what he did so long as he did, were there not widespread support for what he seemed to be *for* and what he seemed to be *against,* no matter how strange Kevorkian is himself. He presented himself as a child of the light, deploying dominant terms of our discourse — "compassion" (let's end suffering now!) and "wants" as "rights." Those opposed to him were children of darkness. He singled out for especial abuse the Catholic Church, medicine, even the press, which, of course, helped to "make" him in the first instance. They would hold things back and stop suffering people from doing what they "wanted" and had a "right" to do in order to end their suffering. Given that a dominant view is that we are all alone with our "rights" by definition (having denied relational personhood), why should we be blocked from exercising that right alone at the end, in a van in a

---

London newspaper that contrasts (to its credit) to much of the media coverage in U.S. newspapers, which tended to take on Kevorkian's own self-congratulatory view of himself as a martyr to a righteous cause. One exception is *The New Republic,* which ran a series of critical pieces on Kevorkian, including his disproportionate selection of women as ideal death-subjects.

27. Daniels, "A Bit of His Own Medicine." Once again one sees how the stuff of dyspotian science fiction yesterday turns into today's proposals and, God forbid, tomorrow's realities.

parking lot somewhere, with the bodies that are the end product being dumped on the doorsteps of hospital emergency rooms or left for police to find? There are many ways to debase the bodies of the ill and dying, and this is surely one.

Perhaps that is why the incarnational dimension has not been altogether quashed. For when people think twice, they blanch before the horrors of a Kevorkian — all the souls who have not forgotten "how to shudder," in Leon Kass's memorable phrase. Ezekiel Emanuel points out that support for "euthanasia and assisted suicide has declined rapidly among those who must administer it"; further, the more people find out about how this actually works, the more they are disinclined to favor changing the laws to sanction the practice. Seventy percent of Michigan voters "opposed a 1998 referendum to legalize assisted suicide."[28] Instead, what people want — and what they wanted all along — was not an absolute right to state-sanctioned death, but more effective ways to *minister to the bodies of the dying.* The public was reflecting a rightful abhorrence at the excessive medicalization of death and the often cruel prolongation of life in a way that in itself constituted an assault on embodied dignity *and* sociality as the dying person was entubed, encased, ensheathed in multiple forms of medical paraphernalia and removed from the tactile world of loved ones. As well, oncologists and other specialists have taken note of their own fears at not being able to "manage" patient pain and suffering and are rethinking how to do that in a way respectful of relational being.

The incarnational moment reasserts itself, as part of what the Pontifical Academy for Life calls "an authentic culture of life, which should . . . accept the reality of the finiteness and natural limits of earthly life. Only in this way can death not be reduced to a

28. Ezekiel J. Emanuel, "Death's Door," *The New Republic,* 17 May 1999, p. 15.

merely clinical event or be deprived of its personal and social dimension."[29] I submit that in the depths of our being, we *know* this. It is an awareness that can be clouded over, go into the shadows, reappear as phantoms and hauntings. But it cannot be altogether quashed. That is why one lingering horror of Nazi genocide is the image of all those bodies, piles of them, being bulldozed into pits once the camps were liberated, being given the closest thing to a decent burial affordable in such desperate circumstances. But we know people deserve better. We know that every single one of these anonymous bodies was somebody's mother, father, son, daughter, wife, husband, child, grandparent, friend. These are the folks by whom we should be accompanied as we move toward death, a surround that speaks to our dignity as persons and that, therefore, puts pressure on excessively clinical, utilitarian, or simply, à la Kevorkian, ghoulish and macabre, approaches to life's end.

Here I want to share our son, Eric's, words at the funeral of his grandfather, my dad, Paul G. Bethke. The words of all the grandchildren were eloquent and powerful. But Eric's serve my purposes particularly well because of the philosophical recognition of incarnate being embedded in them — an awareness of life's palpably incarnate moments, from childhood to death.

> From childhood there are some images: Grandpa feeling a bicep, baiting hooks, pulling weeds, driving a tractor, pulling on and off boots. A small collection, here, and generic in the way childhood memories can be.
>
> It takes adulthood and a great, solemn, pedagogical moment like death and its ceremony to arrange those images in a meaningful way. Gaps are filled in, history paid attention to:

---

29. Pontifical Academy for Life, "The Dignity of Dying People," *Origins* 28, no. 41 (1 April 1999): 707.

new things are dug out of the piles and drawers and boxes of a life's time, and in matching the small, circumstantial evidences of a child with the heavier collecting of being older, a man's life becomes fuller at the moment it is coffined.

When I saw Grandpa the last time, in the corridor of the nursing home he spent his final time in, my mother and I walked him to the common room telling him he'd just seen his family — a large group was visiting that day — and that it was *his* family, *his* doing. "Yes, that's quite a bunch," he said, "that's my gang."

Some of us here can look back and see the history we've made, the gathering of a crowd we've helped along and carefully built. Some of us wait, wishing to do even half as fine a job as Helen and Paul Bethke have done. And now a part of that doing is gone, one Prime Mover has no longer delayed his stay — and his stay, in the small moments of a kid visiting his grandparents in Colorado, to the kind inspections of a thankful, grown grandson — was wonderful, loving, sometimes difficult and, most importantly, filled with the work we must (and hope to) carry on.[30]

Such articulate moments of delicate incarnationality lace and grace much of our lives, and, in our own imperfect ways, we

30. One of the grandchildren's eulogies delivered at the funeral of Paul G. Bethke, who died on September 9, 1993. My dad was in a nursing home in his last months due to advanced Alzheimer's and difficulty managing diabetes. My mom, who died but two years later, also spent her last few years in a facility nearby so it was easier for the family to take turns visiting and tending to each of them. My mother succumbed to a combination of Parkinsonianism and the problems attendant upon therapy for the ailment. The grandchildren also delivered eulogies at her funeral. There are 13 grandchildren; now 7 great-grandchildren, the oldest of whom, JoAnn Paulette Welch, met her great-grandmother before her death. My mom had hoped for a girl as the first great-grandchild.

have devised ritual and ceremony to honor our incarnational comings, goings, and growings. Human ritual is shared incarnationality as persons, together as embodied selves, participate in and create meaning and recognition as the imbricated layers of relationality hum and, at times, burst into song. One ancient and ever new practice along these lines is the pilgrimage. Christians are Augustine's pilgrim people, living amid a bewildering variety of earthly social and political forms, and the journeys of this pilgrim people are to a purpose. The pilgrimage has a transcendent end, but, in the meantime, pilgrims wend their way "along the roads of the world." All are invited to participate in pilgrimage and to see their lives as an "occasion of communion in solidarity with the values of other peoples, brothers and sisters in the humanity that everyone shares and in the common origin of the one Creator of all."[31] A pilgrim puts his or her body on the spot. One cannot be a pilgrim in cyberspace or from the comfort of the den. I recall the words of "Mama Wolejsza" in Warsaw in 1983, on the occasion of John Paul II's second pilgrimage to his homeland as pontiff. Describing the enthusiastic throngs and the spirits of gaiety and overflowing life, hopeful and joyous, she remarked: "You never get tired when you're on pilgrimage."[32]

One of the most powerful instantiations of the incarnational mind in twentieth-century literature is Czeslaw Milosz's classic, *The Captive Mind.* A text that was derided by those still enamored

31. Pontifical Council for Migrants and Travelers, "The Pilgrimage in the Great Jubilee," *Origins* 28, no. 4 (11 June 1998): 53, 59. See also Peter Brown's wonderful book on pilgrimages in the antique Christian community in his *Cult of the Saints* (Chicago: University of Chicago Press, 1981).

32. Our son Eric, then 16, and I followed the pope to many of the sites he visited. We were hosted by Mama Wolejsza and her family in their tiny (by our standards) Warsaw flat. How this all happened is a long and complex tale best reserved for a memoir.

with the world-historical project of Marxism (and in "denial," as we would nowadays say, about Stalinism), it was located by such thinkers as a Cold War polemic. Milosz, who has been a resident of the United States for decades, told me in a conversation that he had been informed by a member of his tenure review committee at Berkeley that he had received tenure *in spite of,* not because of, this great work. What stands out about *The Captive Mind,* a sustained allegory on totalitarianism, is Milosz's determination to be fleshly, concrete, and particular.[33] An incarnational mind and text is a world of concrete presences; it derives from an impulse to make "real" that which is symbolized or represented and the obverse, to symbolize and to represent that which is real. A symbol, a metaphor, a figure does not stand apart from but participates in "the thing-in-itself." The writer or artist or scholar aims neither for a pure realm nor an ideal form but for a way to express reverence for that which *is:* the feel of fresh, cold earth being squeezed through one's fingers on a chilly spring morning; the slosh of cream from a porcelain pitcher as it is poured over a bowl of strawberries; the high-pitched insistent whistle of the tea kettle on the stove; the howls of first one dog, then another, and another, each alone and all together, creating the eerie sensation of lonely, wild animal life in a middle-class neighborhood bereft of people who are all off working. Well, Milosz does this much better than I.

Here, for example, is an extraordinary passage (my favorite) in which Milosz describes walking through a train station in Ukraine in the desperately disordered time of the beginning of World War II. He is caught up short by the following scene:

> A peasant family — husband and wife and two children — had settled down by the wall. They were sitting on baskets and bun-

---

33. I draw here from my essay, "The Incarnational Mind vs. the Captive Mind," *New Oxford Review* 59, no. 8 (October 1992): 12-15.

dles. The wife was feeding the younger child; the husband who had a dark wrinkled face and a black, drooping mustache was pouring tea out of a kettle into a cup for the older boy. They were whispering to each other in Polish. I gazed at them until I felt moved to the point of tears. What had stopped my steps so suddenly and touched me so profoundly was their *difference*. This was a human group, an island in a crowd that lacked something proper to humble, ordinary human life. The gesture of a hand pouring tea, the careful, delicate handing of the cup to the child, the worried words I guessed from the movements of their lips, their isolation, the privacy in the midst of the crowd — that is what moved me. For a moment, then, I understood something that quickly slipped from my grasp.

Perhaps, one might suggest, that "something" concerns the fragility and miracle of the quotidian. Milosz is rightly celebrated for capturing such moments in his poetry, moments that quickly slip or threaten to slip from our grasp. His poems, he tells us, are encounters with the "peculiar circumstances of time and place." This is true as well in *The Captive Mind*. The portrait of that forlorn bit of humanity, huddled together, uprooted, yet making and pouring tea — this, too, says something about the quotidian that can neither be added to nor subtracted from, whether in joy or in terror. For Milosz, one touchstone of the twentieth century (alas) is the terror of the immediacy of stark, physical pain — he is calling to mind the politics of torture and terror. Here I recall the comfort a "mother of the disappeared" from Argentina told me she found in Milosz's passage: "A *living* human being, even if he be thousands of miles away, is not so easily ejected from one's memory. If he is being tortured, his voice is heard at the very least by those who have (uncomfortable as it may be for them) a vivid imagination. And if he is already dead, he is still part of the present; for the man who killed him or who gave the order that he be killed is sitting down somewhere, at some precise point on the face of the earth, with his family; bread and tea are on the table, and his children rejoice over a gift he has brought them."

These words spoke to her of the pain and torture of her own disappeared children; they seemed to gesture toward a humble yet realizable truth. Flannery O'Connor's essay "The Nature and Aim of Fiction" is worth bringing into play. O'Connor writes a powerful brief on behalf of "the concrete" as the distinguishing quality of any fiction worthy of the name. "The beginning of human knowledge is through the senses, and the fiction writer begins where human perception begins. He appeals through the senses, and you cannot appeal to the senses with abstractions. It is a good deal easier for most people to state an abstract idea than to describe and thus re-create some object that they actually see. But the world of the fiction writer is full of matter." It cannot be "unfleshed"; it cannot separate spirit from matter. "The fact is that the materials of the fiction writer are the humblest. Fiction is about everything human and we are made out of dust, and if you scorn getting yourself dusty, then you shouldn't try to write fiction. It's not a grand enough job for you."[34]

O'Connor's comments on dust and grandiosity serve as a bridge to another of Milosz's insistences: warning of the terrible dangers of grand ideologies — any architechtonic schema that scorns the particular, the traditional, the given, and sees human beings as so much raw material to be whipped into some foreordained shape. Powerfully, but with a minimum of didactic and preachy finger-pointing, Milosz apprises us of the terrors of an impositional and invasive "universalism" in the form of an *impe-*

---

34. Flannery O'Connor, "The Nature and Aim of Fiction," in *Mystery and Manners,* ed. Sally and Robert Fitzgerald (New York: Farrar, Straus & Giroux, 1969), pp. 63-86, quotations, pp. 67-68.

rium armed, as was the old Soviet empire, with a sure and certain blueprint for history and a method (dialectical materialism) that could turn the most horrific things (mass slaughter) into the stuff of a future perfect order — or so argued Hannah Arendt.[35] The captive mind is in thrall to such stuff, with its one-dimensional, flattened view of the human being that a totalizing ideology of any kind requires and feeds on. By contrast, the incarnational mind struggles to embody that which is concrete and before us and calls out for recognition, notice, attention.

A third task, then, is to make visible before the world at every moment the fullness, the dignity, the irreducibility, the wonder at creation, the horror, then, at the wanton destruction of creation.

FINALLY, citizens who are Christians and called, therefore, to live in hope *must assure that their churches play a critical role as interpreters of the culture to the culture.* This is a critical civic task. There are few such public sites available, especially in this era of media saturation. Remember the complex position of the Christian as pilgrim, poised between the twin poles of *amor mundi* and *contra mundum.* This means one is gifted with the task to transform a wounded culture — not as a messianic project but as a work of grace and love. In recognizing and holding ever before our eyes the dignity of the human person created in God's image, one is called to articulate and to work to achieve a common good, not as enforced homogeneity but as a type of community that turns on and recognizes the particular gifts each brings to the banquet table of life.

In a presentation by Francis Cardinal George delivered May 9, 1998, on "Society and the Mission of the Laity," the cardinal,

---

35. Hannah Arendt, *On Violence* (New York: Harcourt, Brace and World, 1970).

having noted that it is "very difficult to talk about the common good in America" because we think all there is to do is to "negotiate particular interests" and rely on the law to "bear the entire burden of unity," went on to insist that one cannot "evangelize what you don't love." The work of the church as interpreter is a work of love. One cannot hate that which one would transform. There is something good in every culture. It would be astonishing were this not so; indeed, I would say it would be impossible because that would mean that that culture had been denuded utterly of any access to the good, that it was living in a barren wilderness of the spirit.

Yet so many of our cultural critics seem to despise American culture or to have given up hope for it entirely. If, at one point, this seemed the purview of the left — with its violent negations of all things "Amerikan" — now such voices are heard more from the right of center. America is construed as one seething fleshpot ready to implode. The voice that prevails is that of condemnation. But if the culture were really beyond redemption, it would cast doubts on creation itself and its goodness. Surely that cannot be bleached out entirely! Let's look at a few signs of the times cultural critics (rightly) point to as evidence of disorder or moral catatonia but read these signs in a more hopeful way, following an Augustinian commitment to charitable interpretation.

To start things off, we know, for example, that children do better, all other things being equal, in two-parent households. On every index of child well-being this is so. Two-parent households are no guarantee of child well-being, but the risks for children rise dramatically — and this holds when one controls for socioeconomic and educational status — in single-parent, primarily single-mother, households. So we are dealing with widespread fatherlessness. A situation to be lamented for many reasons, to be sure. But why create straw men and women and come up with theories that denounce all men as feckless, though some are surely, or all women as selfish sexual adventurers, though some surely are? (Depending on one's political perspective, one or the other of these canards pops up with depressing frequency.) Instead, why not look at the fact that the bleak evidence on what happens when families are stripped of a central feature of sociality and relationality is a portent that we are born to relationship and community; that we have nothing to prove as stalwart individualists; that fathers and mothers are *needed* by children; that what we (or many of us) were taught as children is true and reliable, something we can build on. Through this more charitable hermeneutical exercise, one would change the direction, moving from punitive measures *against* single parenting to positive and generous measures to sustain often stressed two-parent child-rearing households.[36]

Another issue that continues to inspire something akin to despair — deeply and ardently felt — and, at times, the most severe language of condemnation is the current abortion regime. But a charitable interpretation would point to hopeful signs, including the fact that the latest reliable surveys indicate that over 70 percent of Americans think access to abortion should be limited in some circumstances. Only 16 percent of the public think abor-

36. I realize this just skims the surface of this matter. There are hundreds of books on the subject, many of them terrible, unfortunately — terrible in the sense of repeating hoary nostrums and reincoding debasing ideologies whether woman-as-victim or man-as-villain or the like. Especially distressing are those that claim the child's needs for nurture are entirely social constructions and inventions, as if children could rear themselves. See, for example, Aminatta Forna, *Mother of All Myths: How Society Molds and Constrains Mothers* (New York: HarperCollins, 1999). The best book on the effects of fatherlessness is Sara McClanahan and Gary Sandifer, *Growing up with a Single Parent: What Hurts, What Helps* (Cambridge: Harvard University Press, 1994). Works by David Blankenhorn and David Poponoe are also recommended. Blankenhorn, Jean Bethke Elshtain, and Steven Bayme, *Rebuilding the Nest* (Milwaukee: Family Services Publication, 1990), is a useful collection.

tion should be illegal under all circumstances; some 27 percent that abortions should be permitted in all circumstances. Interestingly enough, however, the number of people who call themselves "pro-choice" has dropped since the triumph of what many have called an "abortion culture" in the wake of *Roe v. Wade.* The number identifying themselves as pro-life has risen.[37] Working with such figures, one can patiently and charitably engage strong pro-choicers and ask them to explore their own moral queasiness about an unlimited abortion right — as we have evidence that such is widespread. Doesn't this perhaps speak to a deep uneasiness about narrowing the boundary of moral concern where human life in utero at any stage of development is concerned? Shouldn't Christians live out an alternative by showing a generous concern for all lives of all children, born and unborn? Shouldn't this voice and concrete, hands-on programs of help and nurture prevail? When we note how many enthusiastic American young people themselves went on pilgrimage to greet John Paul II at the World Youth Convocation in Denver, Colorado, a few years back — hundreds of thousands, filled with hope and vigor and joy in life — can we really despair of our culture? They went to be with one another, and they went because they revere John Paul's holiness and courage and integrity, and, so they tell us, there are so few examples of such for them to emulate. We know — we have strong evidence that this is so — that examples of adult integrity and plain, straightforward talk to teenagers help them to make critical decisions, including refraining from pregnancy and childbearing until they are older and living in a sustaining relationship. Let's build on that.

Yet another area in which hard voices of condemnation too often prevail is an engagement with the world of the pop-

37. Richard Benedetto, "Abortion Poll Reflects Public's Deep Divisions," *USA Today,* Wednesday, May 5, 1999, p. 15A.

therapeutic, the overly eager search for whatever will make me feel better and feel that way all the time. The coming of what has been called the "Prozac culture" is what I have in mind: that millions of prescriptions are written for people who are not clinically depressed but just want to "perform" at peak efficiency or never to have a "down moment" in their lives. At present, calmer voices from within psychiatry and medicine are issuing cautions about this psychic version of our flight from finitude. If churches would uphold clearly a vision of the integrity of human life and finitude, including our entirely predictable moments of weariness, anger, perplexity, and grief, and treat this as part of our dignity and complexity as persons, perhaps we would be less driven to seek cure-alls. The huge expansion in psychiatric services and the enormous, jelly-like expanding category of "mental illness" gives one pause.

But the culture-hating response is to thump persons who claim to have such needs and to condemn the mental health establishment in toto. A more generous approach is to sustain a serious, theologically grounded discussion of the nature of human happiness, and human restlessness, and the pain and excision of selves that comes from loneliness and isolation — a condition our culture often seems to mandate if one wants to "prove" one can "go it alone." As psychiatrist Paul Crichton noted recently, doctors should "not be seduced into prescribing happiness, as some of Prozac's frenzied advocates have urged them to do, as this would reveal not only therapeutic megalomania, but a profound misunderstanding of the true nature of happiness."[38] The church as interpreter must continue to represent the restlessness of the human heart, its needs and hungers, and the places where it finds nourishment, beauty, peace, and, finally, rest.

38. Paul Crichton, "A prescription for happiness?" *Times Literary Supplement,* July 2, 1999, p. 14.

My last example of the church and Christians as cultural hermeneuts is from the arena of popular cinema. Movies have been taking lots of hits from critics recently, and for good reason. Much of what is out there is either pap or authentically degrading, representing human beings at their most debased, hideous, selfish, and cruel, as entertainment for profit. I am here thinking not of serious films, like Steven Spielberg's *Schindler's List,* which necessarily depicts Nazi cruelty and debasement, but instead of so many of the horrifically stupid and graphically violent "entertainments" put out for consumption by teenagers. But there is much else going on. Blanket targeting of films that display *any* violence simply falls wide of the mark and suggests to many young people (and not they alone) that Christians are heremetically sealed-off grumps.

Consider the 1995 film *Seven* that many "Christian" voices enjoined people not to see because it graphically depicted the aftermath of grotesque murders. (We do not actually see the murders committed but we see pictorial representations of these murders in most instances, thankfully not in the final murder.) What hits Detective Somerset (Morgan Freeman) right from the start is that the first murder is an "act that has meaning." He knows the murders are just beginning. Why? Because of the methodical, deliberate nature of what was done and how it was done, with the word GLUTTONY scrawled in grease on the kitchen wall of an obese man who had been forced to eat himself to death. Detective Somerset, in his quest to understand, cites Milton. He predicts that six more murders will come. His brash young partner, just assigned to this detective division, Detective Mill (Brad Pitt), is impatient and finds Somerset unintelligible, a little loony himself. The killer is "just a psycho," a crazy who pees all over himself and blabs nonsense. Somerset knows it is far more serious. He himself haunts the public library after closing hours (he is friends with the night custodial crew and watchmen). He begins to reread and to consult Dante's *Purgatorio* and Chaucer's *Canterbury Tales*. He consults the *Dictionary of Catholicism*. He recommends these to Mill. Almost crazy with impatience, Mill throws away Dante, having tried without success to read it — the dominant Western tradition with its reflections on questions of good, evil, Satan, God, theodicy elude Mill entirely. He is a child of the media era: he bounces around erratically, says "whatever" a lot, and resorts to Cliff Notes versions.

Cliff Notes — the film suggests that that is the way our culture at present knows its great traditions, if at all: through a summary outline in which all the work has been done by others. One no longer has the patience to do the hard work of learning. One has lost access to a yet vibrant and enriching wellspring of human knowledge, identity, complexity, and purpose.

If Monday's murder was GLUTTONY, Tuesday's is GREED. A wealthy lawyer has bled to death, forced to cut off one pound of his own flesh. The *Merchant of Venice* is the relevant textual reference point. Somerset notes that this leaves SLOTH, WRATH, PRIDE, LUST, and ENVY to go. It will continue.

The film plays out in a kind of inferno. It is always raining, gray, bleak. Sidewalks are dirty. Paint peels off walls. There is no color save a kind of brownish, greenish, grayish — colors of decay. Somerset muses that the murders are like "forced contrition." The victim is contrite not because he or she has come to "love God" but because he or she is forced to undergo a violent expiation and is then killed. Mill is agog with disbelief at Somerset's hermeneutical strategy and approach. The murderer has left a message at the GREED murder scene: "Help Me." Mill interprets this as just another sicko whimpering. He bleaches the meaning out of all the signs. Somerset, mordantly, describes the task he and Mill are undertaking in general as homicide detectives: We are picking up the pieces. Putting things in neat piles. So many corpses unrevenged.

By Thursday, they think they have a fingerprint match to the killer, or so the signs tell them. But no, they have been faked out. The seven-deadly-sins killer has cut off the hand of a victim whom he has kept methodically and cruelly tied up for over a year, even to the point of using antibiotics for any bladder infections, in order that he can, through forced inactivity, display the contrition attendant upon SLOTH. The severed hand provides the fingerprints that lead the police to a room where, bound to a bed, is a rotting, barely alive corpselike entity, starved and effectively brain dead. Somerset keeps thinking. He is deeply frightened; the killer has purpose. Somerset focuses on the details. He is playing a complex game. At this point, Mill's beautiful young wife, Tracy (Gwyneth Paltrow), meets with Somerset, a sympathetic, older African-American gentleman of the "old school," just to have someone to talk to. She hates the drab, decaying world they find themselves in. She cannot bear the elementary schools she has visited (she was a fifth grade teacher "upstate") — they are such terrible environments for children. She is lonely, sad, and she is pregnant, but she has not told her husband. Somerset, trying not to advise, nevertheless tells her if he had it to do over again, he would have the child he succeeded in urging the woman he never quite married to abort. There is not a day that passes, he tells Tracy, that he does not regret that decision. "Spoil the kid every chance you get," he urges Tracy, steering her in the direction of life.

In the meantime, the meticulous killer goes about his work. Somerset says, "These murders are his sermons to us." Mill is incredulous. "The guy's a whack job." Saturday turns up the death labeled LUST. A woman has died horribly in a sexual act into which her partner, the precipitate cause of her horrible, painful death by evisceration, was coerced at pain of his own death. Somerset warns Mill: "This isn't going to have a happy ending," and notes that "Satan himself couldn't live up to the expectations that are building," for the killer will be "just a man," here revisiting the theme of evil as diminished, not grand.[39] Wearily, Somerset notes that he is tired of living in a place that "nurtures apathy as a virtue." Sunday is the murder designated as PRIDE, a beautiful woman whose nose has been "cut off to spite her face." Astonishingly, at this point the killer, bloodied, shows up at police headquarters to turn himself in to Somerset and Mill. He has already had one shoot-out with them, for they had tracked him down to his apartment through the signs he has left everywhere given the books he has checked out: you are what you read.

Some read the works the killer has absorbed as a way to think of the theodicy question and as object lessons in what happens to human being itself absent a transcendent reference point. The killer has made himself his own point of reference. He claims that he was "chosen." Somerset challenges him, noting that "if your hand was forced, you shouldn't enjoy it." A real messiah does not exult and gloat. The killer is proud of his death-dealing tasks and proclaims their necessity — he was wiping out people who embodied deadly sins. They were not "innocent." Of course, in Christian theology, none of us is. The killer confidently predicts that what he is doing will be "followed forever." He is the arbiter of life and death.

Having taken the two detectives to a barren desert wasteland, where the sun is glaring brutally and all is empty, he awaits the end result of his grotesque, cruel handiwork. It comes in the form of a box that contains the severed head of Tracy, Mill's wife. (We do not see this. We see only the look of horror — a soul-shuddering moment — as Somerset opens the box, while Mill

---

39. See my discussion of Augustine and Hannah Arendt on this issue in *Augustine and the Limits of Politics* (Notre Dame: Notre Dame University Press, 1996).

guards the murderer.) The killer starts to describe his handiwork to Mill. Somerset is screaming for Mill to drop his gun. He doesn't want the chain of violence to continue. The killer taunts Mill — he, the killer, was overtaken by ENVY of Mill and his life and his wife, so he "took her pretty head," and he must die at the hands of Mill, who is now made WRATH. Somerset cries out to Mill, "He wants you to shoot him." Mill is to embody WRATH. Please, Somerset begs, if you kill him, he will win. Mill, twisted and screaming in pain and disbelief, crying No! No! shoots the eagerly anticipatory killer once, then empties his gun.

Evil has won. The film ends with a voice-over by Somerset: "Ernest Hemingway once wrote, 'The world is a fine place and worth fighting for.' I agree with the first part." We are left drained. The cycle of vengeance goes on. Perhaps the most wounded victim in this gallery of grotesque deaths is Mill, who will go on living, knowing he has enacted the killer's last "sermon." But the film is an allegory on what happens when signs have lost their meaning — to all but Somerset, who cannot get things on an interpretive track intelligible to others because they have lost access to the tradition of thinking about good and evil. A critical hermeneutic would see here on display a twisted theodicy and the defamed fruits of cruel self-absorption of a particularly megalomaniacal sort. That our culture seems to throw up more and more such representations — and living exemplars — should be a matter of deep concern. The response should be loving regard and a recognition that hope yet shines its steady light. But we must push back the scrim of darkness to see it.

Think here of the horror of the Columbine School massacres and the shocked lamentations that succeeded it — proof positive, to some, that young people were going to hell. Two young men were certainly in hell, captured by the darkness and representations of evil, and they struck out, targeting explicitly, at least in several instances, students who voiced their belief in the God of creation. Some of the wounded were shot, they tell us, because they said they believed and were carrying Bibles. Rachel Scott was shot first in the leg and then through the head when she said she believed in God. Cassie Bernall, having answered yes to the question, "Do you believe in God?" was shot through the temple.[40] Who can imagine such courage under such terrible circumstances? But look what students did during the course of the massacre and after: at risk to their own lives they ushered frantic and paralyzed classmates to safety. (This is how one young man died.) They struggled to keep their coach and teacher, Dave Sanders, alive, staunching his wounds with their torn t-shirts, fashioning a stretcher from table legs; and when it was clear he was bleeding to death, they held him and prayed with and for him and showed him pictures of his family. They created prayer circles as the siege continued. They loved and cared for one another. In the aftermath, they put up signs and crosses and offered prayers and devout promises to help to rebuild a community that would constitute a living memorial to their classmates who had perished. This is, to put it bluntly, a hell of a thing for kids to go through. But the way in which these young people went through it should help us to savor living hope rather than to dwell exclusively on the violence and to lament and condemn all things adolescent.

Back, briefly, to the culture of films. It is the top-grossing film of all time, *Titanic,* that I want to explore in closing. Titanic was a cultural event of, well, titanic proportions, with huge throngs going week after week, men and women of all ages and in every country in which it played. What were they by the millions coming for? Many cultural critics put it off entirely on "chick flick" teen enthusiasm for the (admittedly) extraordinary young actor, Leonardo di Caprio, who plays the self-sacrificing protagonist,

40. There are now debates on whether this *really* happened. Certainly something like this did, given the eye and ear witnesses.

Jack Dawson, the film's romantic lead. But this misses the boat (again, if you will forgive me). Viewers told of being "drawn back to" the film again and again. Experts were dumbfounded, with 40 percent of those who had seen it wanting to see it again — compared with 2 percent for the average film. More than a third of the audience was over 25. Graves of Titanic victims were thronged in a popular pilgrimage never imagined possible to cemeteries in Halifax, Nova Scotia, where a number of the Titanic dead are buried, including one "Jack Dawson," the name of the film's hero. What was — is — going on here?

I have tried this interpretation out a few times and it was not regarded as crazy, so let me unpack it up as another example of how the Christian tradition affords symbolically and conceptually lush interpretive sites for dominant cultural phenomena. What *Titanic* offers is a penetrating view of the cost of human arrogance and pride. The villain, one Caledon Hockley (Billy Zane), gloats that "God himself could not sink this ship." Even the name "Titanic" can be construed as a kind of thumbing one's nose at divinity. The titans, after all, were underworld destroyers who, if unleashed, did nothing but wreak havoc. Mr. Ismay, the ship's builder (not her architect, Mr. Andrews, who was a decent man) extols the mechanical brilliance of the ship's supremacy — it was "willed into solid reality." Sheer size is proclaimed a good in itself. And, from prideful arrogance, an insufficient number of lifeboats have been installed, it having been considered a waste of good deck space to put in a number that could accommodate all passengers. Why bother, as no one would ever be *in need of saving;* all were already rescued, so to speak, being on an unsinkable ship.

The film veers back and forth between life in steerage and the world of the upper class. (And the rich were very rich indeed, this being in the days before a graduated income tax.) So the ship that cannot sink moves over the glassy sea. On the upper decks all is diamonds, furs, shimmer, and glamour as privilege closes ranks and every whim is catered to by a huge, properly obsequious staff. Beneath her decks is a blazing inferno as giant boilers roar, and engines — the biggest ever on a ship — grind and roar, exuding evidence of power. A transgressive love affair builds between Rose DeWitt Bukater (upper class) and Jack Dawson (American, steerage, a good-hearted itinerant artist living on "God's good humor") who understands that "life's a gift. You never know what you're going to be dealt." One must, therefore, "make each day count." Everyone knows the story as a sustained allegory on human chance and the hideous fruits of pride that strike most deeply into the company of the less privileged, with Hockney proclaiming, in response to Rose's cry that there are sufficient lifeboats for only half, that half *must* die, "Not the better half."

Jack and Rose cling together: "If you jump, I jump." The film shows acts of cowardice, chicanery, stupidity, grace. Some comport themselves with dignity and sacrifice themselves for others, including "lesser" sorts. The ship of dreams has turned into a sinking horror with intimations of all that is best and ample scope for all that is lowest about us. A priest prays the rosary with others who cling to him. "I saw a new heaven and a new earth . . . the former world had passed away." The band plays "Nearer My God to Thee" and perishes, comforting people till the end — an act that can be taken as folly or grace, depending on one's interpretive site. Jack saves Rose. "I've got you. I won't let go." He pleads with her to "Do me this honor. Promise you'll survive. Promise you won't give up." He gives up his life for her as the door fragment afloat on the icy water would capsize were more than one person to attempt to occupy it. Fifteen hundred human beings went into the sea; only six were pulled to safety. Boats floated away only partially full.

Now I have heard complaints from a Christian perspective

that the film contains a pernicious message as Rose describes Jack as having "saved her" in "all the ways a human being can be saved." She says this as an old woman remembering her experience, recalling the way she was slated for an endless "parade of balls and cotillions" and witless chatter as the rich reveled in, well, their richness. The "ship of dreams" was, for her, a slave ship taking her into a forced marriage to an arrogant man of means who believed he could buy anything, including life and death. As life merges into death at the film's beginning with its underwater images of the ship's forlorn, majestic ruin, at the film's end the dead are powerfully reborn in a new life on a very different Titanic. Rose dreams and the dream is paradisiacal: the ship is recreated, alive once more; there is beauty and music and camaraderie, and in her transformed vision those separated by status and office are all together, brought together in a great circle above and at the base of the grand staircase in order to bless a young love. It is a dream of reunion, people gathered without distinction, reminiscent of the communion scene in *Places in the Heart,* where the sheriff and his young killer take communion side by side, and those who have been parted by violence and fear are reunited under the sign of Christ's sacrifice and God's grace.

We do well not to minimize or mock or belittle these moments. They speak to a hunger and a search for meaning and grace. Although Rose utters what can be taken as heretical — Jack cannot save her in *all* the ways a human being can be saved, surely — she also embodies, with words and in a dream, the transcendent reference point she cannot fully articulate, or chooses not to. In discussing those who, like Ismay, saved themselves and debased themselves in so doing as so many children from steerage went to desperate, watery deaths, Rose comments that he and those like him were "waiting for an absolution that would never come," certainly not if they hoped to absolve themselves of such selfishness and pride. But it is her imagined dream of reunion and ingathering that is so powerful. We are struck because the single most powerful way to read it is as a vision of the kingdom of heaven where all are gathered together, where *ressentiment* is known no more. The poor have not replaced the rich or the captain or others of power in her dream; instead, all have been mixed up *and* joined together, and they are united precisely because *they are focused on something other than themselves; they are united in and through Jack and Rose's love.* This is not enough for our hungry hearts. But earthly love affords intimations of the love that passes all understanding, glimpses of what a community of love and a God who so loved the world is all about. We still see through a glass darkly but, if we push just a bit, the film, charitably interpreted, helps us to see more and deeper. The reason so many kept returning is that *they wanted to understand why they were returning.* The film was nurture of some sort. What need, what good, was here hinted at even if in cinematic and at times nigh-melodramatic form?[41] Read the signs of the times. Love the world enough to want to know it. Know the world enough to love it.

Despite it all — the troubles, the pain, the frustrations, the dangers of self-pride or excessive self-abnegation — through it all trust, hope, and, for Christians, the greatest of all: love. Let us add thankfulness, gratitude, to this list. One of our grandsons, dear Bobby, now three, said to me when he was just barely two and I was swinging him in the backyard on a sunny, crisp day as

---

41. Even a film like *The Matrix,* much condemned in the wake of Columbine High School, points to that which it cannot itself make manifest. The film is riddled with violence, yes, but there is talk of the "One" and of "Zion" and of getting out of a world in which one is forced to live falsely. The theology, however, is very weak. A chosen one does not become such at the moment he begins to "believe in himself." This is a very New Age, pop-psych substitute for serious theology. But it is a cut above the standard slasher, bomber, action film.

a slight breeze stirred the leaves in the trees: "Everything is everywhere." This said as he looked at me after having gazed for a time at the sun, the rustling leaves, the expanse of yard, a cat frolicking nearby: *everything is everywhere*. It is that childlike awe and wonder, in words as beautiful to me as any I have ever heard, that is the warp and woof of hope and love. Delight and wonder are part and parcel of hope and trust; for without hope and trust our hearts are locked away, as Augustine would say. He was right.

II. MATTHEW 6:9-13

Blue herons that fish in silence,
webs that sag with dew,
old pines in mist,
the snow at sea,
and hues as they merge in evening,
rain on mossed rocks,
and crackling flames,
and a breeze touched with brine,
and leaf-stained light in autumn,
Gandhi, Bach, Monet, Maria,
and a stream pool laved with pollen,
the surf as it lathers
and then hisses on the beaches,
the twilight, the stillness

*   :these things*

FRED DINGS,
from *After the Solstice*
(reprinted with permission of the author)

Index

Abortion: Christian responses to, 97, 115; distortion of language and, 132; public opinion concerning, 156-57; relation to sloth, 85, 97, 99; Roe v. Wade, 96-97, 157; of "special needs" children, 96

Adam. *See* Genesis

Advertising, 39-40, 52

Aggiornamento, 6

Andersen, Kurt, 109-11

Anselm, Saint, 140

Aquinas, Saint Thomas, 12

Arendt, Hannah, 134-35, 137, 154

Augustine, Saint, 12, 42, 43, 46, 53-54, 60, 62-63, 138, 150, 169

Babies: adoption of, 51; cloning and, 103; sale of, 49-51; teen pregnancy, 64. *See also* Children

Barth, Karl, 83-84

Bladerunner, 7

Bodies: Bonhoeffer and, 129-30; Christian conception of, 14-16, 25-30, 143; church as body of Christ, 129; limitations of embodiment, 89, 97-98, 121, 129-30; nuptial meaning of, 30; relation to the self, 16, 27, 131, 150. *See also* Abortion; Christian; Cloning; Genetic Engineering; Rea-soning Capacity; Repugnance; Sexuality; Shame

Body parts: sale of, 48-50

Bolt, Robert, 6

Bonhoeffer, Dietrich: on community, 128-29; ethics of, 2, 48, 114-16, 118, 135-37; on freedom, 43, 86; in historical context, 10-13; on pride, 39, 43, 72-73; theological anthropology of, 13-24, 58, 60; theological comparison with John Paul II, 30-35; writings of, 3-4, 46. Works: *Creation and Fall,* 12; *Ethics,* 114-16; *Letters and Papers from Prison,* 12; *Life Together,* 128

Book of Common Prayer, 121-22

Brave New World, 110

Brown, Peter, 43

Buck v. Bell, 100

Burnell, Peter, 62

Camus, Albert, 119-20, 140-41

Capote, Truman, 118

Captive Mind, The, 150-53

Carlson, Allan, 66

Catholic: church, 146; perspectives on cloning, 104; social thought, 35, 72-75; theology, 11, 35, 60, 85. *See also* John Paul II; Christian

Children: Down's syndrome, 94-96; marketing aimed at, 40, 52; parental love of, 63-72, 81-82; sale of, 48-50; single parenting of, 155-56; "special needs" category, 95-96; time required for, 57, 65-72; truth and, 136-37; violence of, 64, 163-64. *See also* Babies; Abortion

Children of Men, The, 122-23

Christ: community and, 167; Hegel's conception of, 140; love of neighbor and, 130; theological understanding of 14, 21, 31, 42, 140. *See also* Bonhoeffer; Christian; Jesus of Nazareth; John Paul II

Christian: being-in-the-world, 143-44; hope, 5, 11, 127, 141; influence on philosophy, 4-6, 10, 49, 57; interpretations of culture, 154-69; opposition to the death penalty, 121; participation in community, 62, 129-30; perspectives on films, 159-68; pilgrims, 83, 150; redemption, 26, 42; reflection on the economy, 53-54, 59-60, 72-73; servanthood, 84. *See also* Bonhoeffer; John Paul II

Cloning: of animals: 101; ethics of, 100-103, 105, 107, 108; federal government and, 101; of humans, 100-102, 104; religious perspectives on, 104

Columbine High School, 64, 163-64. *See also* Children: violence

Commodification: limitations on, 44-59, 73-75, 77. *See also* Consumerism; Economics

Common good, 73

Communion: of persons, 28-30; *in communio,* 22, 32, community and, 150

Community: of belief, 6; Catholic social thought on, 74; Christian understandings of, 62, 128-30, 143; cyberspace and, 128-32; pride as destructive of, 41, 44; prerequisites for, 18, 40, 62, 65; relationality and, 60, 62, 143-44, 156; support of families, 68, 97. *See also* Bonhoeffer; John Paul II

Consumerism: community and, 39-41; limitations on commodification, 44-59, 73-75, 77; Christian responses to, 42-44, 52-54, 57-63, 72-75, 77. *See also* Economics

Consumption, 39-41, 52. *See also* Consumerism; Economics

Conventionalism, 48. *See also* Social Constructivism

Crichton, Paul, 158

Culture: Christian interpretation of, 154-68; idolatry and, 32; psychiatric therapy and, 157-58

Daniels, Anthony, 146

Darwin, 10, 16

Death penalty: Christian perspectives on, 115; cultural images of, 118-19; deterrence and, 119-20; ethics of, 115-21; link to culture, 85

Dick, Phillip K., 7

Dings, Fred, 1, 37, 79, 125, 170

Do Androids Dream of Electric Sheep?, 7

Economics: ethical analysis of, 34-35, 39-77, 138. *See also* Commodification; Consumerism; Utility

Eliade, Mircea, 12

Elohist account. *See* Genesis 1:27

Emotivism, 106

Eugenics movement, 91, 100, 104

Euthanasia, 99, 115, 132, 145-47

Eve. *See* Genesis

Faith: fideism as, 138-39; reason and, 137-40; religious, 4, 43, 48, 60

Faron, Theodore, 122-23

Freedom: as abandoned out of sloth, 77, 88, 95-97, 99, 101-3; as distorted by pride, 39, 42-44; as faithfulness to the natural order, 86-87; in Genesis account, 16; language and, 132; movements, 11; as relationship, 14-15, 29-30

Freud, Sigmund, 12

Gattaca, 93-94

Genesis: theological interpretation of, 10, 12-34, 113-15. *Specific references:* Genesis book one, 13; Genesis (1:27), 13-14, 22-24; Genesis book two, 16, 24, 32; Genesis (2:24), 14-15, 16, 22-24, 32; Genesis (3:15), 26; Genesis (4:1), 33

Genetic engineering: for enhancement, 89-92, 98; ethical analysis of, 79, 81-123; false account of body in, 97-98, 130; fictional accounts of, 7-9, 93-94, 108-11, 122-23; for medical reasons, 91,

99; sale of genetic material, 90-94; xenotransplantation, 106-12. *See also* Cloning; Human Genome Project

George, Francis Cardinal, 154-55

Gilbert, Walter, 90

Gnosticism, 131, 145

Gunton, Colin, 113-14, 144

Havel, Václav, 105

Hegel, Georg Friedrich, 140-41

Heidegger, Martin, 12

Hemingway, Ernest, 163

Hobbes, Thomas, 10, 83, 117-18, 144

Hope, 5-6, 11, 127, 133, 139, 141, 142, 150, 168. *See also* Christian

Horton Hatches the Eggs, 81-82

Human Genome Project, 89-90, 130. *See also* Cloning; Genetic Engineering

I Want to Live!, 119

Ideology, 47, 55, 153. *See also* Consumerism

Imago dei, 19, 26, 28, 117

In Cold Blood, 118

Involuntary sterilization, 92

Island of Dr. Moreau, 108

James, P. D., 122-23

Jesus of Nazareth, 22, 30-31. *See also* Christ

John Paul II: Catholic social thought and, 73-74; critique of consumer culture, 45, 48, 52-53; ethics of, 48, 112-13, 116-18, 120, 138-40; historical context of, 10-12; on love, 2; as role model,

150, 157; theological anthropology of, 22-35, 39, 43, 58, 60, 62, 77, 112-14; theology of the body, 23, 25, 29, 30. Works: *Fides et Ratio,* 138, *Catechesis on the Book of Genesis,* 22
Johnson, Samuel, 127
Jonas, Hans, 104
Jung, C. G., 12

Kant, Immanuel, 135-39
Kass, Leon, 106-7, 147
Kevorkian, Jack, 59, 145-48
King, Martin Luther, 56
Knowledge of good and evil, 16-19, 24-25, 35, 163. *See also* Faith; Genesis; Reasoning Capacity
Kolata, Gina, 101
Kuttner, Robert, 54-55, 57-58

Language: ethical implications of, 57, 88, 95, 128, 132, 139, 143-46; truth and, 133-37; universal, 14
Leach, William, 40-41
Levinas, Emmanuel, 12
Levy-Bruhl, Lucien, 12
Locke, John, 144
Long, D. Stephen, 53
Love, 29, 34, 43, 63, 77, 140, 168. *See also* Children; Christian
Lovin, Robin, 86-87
Luther: assessment of human fallenness by, 21, 27, 31, 39, 58, 60, 84-85; on Christian faith, 68; on Christian freedom, 86; on church as body of Christ, 129; on sloth, 77, 82-83. Works: *On the Bondage of the Will,* 21; *The*

Freedom of a Christian, 86; *Small Catechism,* 35
Lutheran, 11, 60, 72-73. *See also* Bonhoeffer; Christian

Man for All Seasons, 6
Marriage, 30, 32, 61-62
Martyrdom, 11, 164
Marx, Karl, 46, 113, 151; dialectical materialism of, 154
Mary, mother of Jesus, 21, 32-33
Matthew (19:3ff.), 22, 26; Matthew (6:9-13), 170
Milosz, Czeslaw, 150-53
Money: appeal of, 46, 89; desocializing effect of, 45; preoccupation with, 44, 141. *See also* Consumerism; Economics
More, Thomas, 6

Nazism, 10-11, 92, 100, 115, 129, 135, 145, 148, 159
Nietzsche, Friedrich, 12, 17
Nihilism, 44
Nominalism, 48

Objective: limits, 18; meaning and truth, 48, 113, 143; reality, 23, 139
O'Connor, Flannery, 153
O'Donovan, Oliver, 116-17
Ontological, 14, 23, 25, 29, 112, 139

Paleontology, 141-42
Peloponnesian War, 133
Personhood, 143-45
Places in the Heart, 167
Plato, 12

Paul VI, 113
Pride: consumer culture and, 52; disguised as freedom, 39, 42, 44; philosophical, 56; relation to sloth, 35, 77, 83-85, 88, 120; sociality and, 63, 72; theological conceptions of, 42-44, 104; in *Titanic,* 165, 167; *See also* Chapter 2 (entire)
Public choice theory, 55-56

Radin, Margaret Jane, 48-50
Reasoning capacity: as embodied, 87, 106; human fallenness and, 21, 25, 26, 31, 85; limits on, 19, 29, 85, 137-42. *See also* Christian; Knowledge of good and evil; Freedom; Genesis
Repugnance: wisdom of, 106-7. *See also* Kass; Xenotransplantation
Ressourcement, 5
Ricoeur, Paul, 12
Robinson, Marilynne, 54
Roman Catholic. *See* Catholic
"Ron's Angels," 91

Sartre, Jean-Paul, 113
Scheler, Max, 12
Schindler's List, 159
Schmitz, Kenneth L., 143
Seed, Richard, 104-5
Seuss, Dr., 81-82
Seven, 159-63
Sexuality, 18, 32, identity and, 27; post-Fall misuses, 20; sale of, 49, 51. *See also* Bodies; John Paul II; Shame
Shame, 18, 20, 29, 32, 47
Sinsheimer, Robert, 100

Slavery: cloning and, 104; contrasted with Christian servanthood, 84; economics and, 54-55; Hegelian master/slave dialectic, 18, 84; right to life and, 8, 116
Sloth: as denial of finitude, 88, 99; fictional depiction of, 81-82; reason as crippled by, 106, 120-21; relation to pride, 35, 77, 83-84, 88, 120; as self-abnegation, 84-85; theological conceptions of, 82-84. *See also* Chapter 3 (entire); Christian; Economics; Genetic Engineering
Slouka, Mark, 130
Smith, Adam, 47
Social constructivism, 48, 139
Spielberg, Steven, 159
Stalinism, 10, 151. *See also* Totalitarianism
Starkweather, Charles, 118, 120
Subjective definition of man, 23
Subjectivism, 23, 101, 112-14, 143
Subjectivity, 113

Taylor, Charles, 143
Thucydides, 133
Tillich, Paul, 12
Titanic (ship), 46
Titanic (film), 164-68
Totalitarianism, 11, 128, 133-34, 151
Tribe, Laurence, 102
Trinitarian concept of God, 28, 143. *See also* Christian; Community
Turn of the Century, 109-11

Universalism, 153
Utilitarian, 48
Utilitarianism, 146, 148
Utility: maximization, 55-59; as
   principle of value, 44, 53

Wilson, James Q., 131
Wittgenstein, Ludwig, 55
Wojtyla, Karol. *See* John Paul II
World War I, 134-35

World War II, 10, 151-52

Xenotransplantation, 106-12. *See
   also* Cloning; Genetic Engineering

Yahwist account. *See* Genesis (2:24)

Zallen, Doris T., 92